Marilyn

PUBLIC ACCOUNTABILITY:

EVALUATING TECHNOLOGY-BASED INSTITUTIONS

PUBLIC ACCOUNTABILITY:

EVALUATING TECHNOLOGY-BASED INSTITUTIONS

Albert N. Link
Department of Economics
University of North Carolina at Greensboro

John T. Scott
Department of Economics
Dartmouth College

KLUWER ACADEMIC PUBLISHERS
BOSTON / DORDRECHT / LONDON

Distributors for North, Central and South America:
Kluwer Academic Publishers
101 Philip Drive
Assinippi Park
Norwell, Massachusetts 02061 USA
Telephone (781) 871-6600
Fax (781) 871-6528
E-Mail <kluwer@wkap.com>

Distributors for all other countries:
Kluwer Academic Publishers Group
Distribution Centre
Post Office Box 322
3300 AH Dordrecht, THE NETHERLANDS
Telephone 31 78 6392 392
Fax 31 78 6546 474
E-Mail <orderdept@wkap.nl>

Electronic Services <http://www.wkap.nl>

Library of Congress Cataloging-in-Publication Data

A C.I.P. Catalogue record for this book is available from the Library of Congress.

Printed on acid-free paper.

Printed in the United States of America

For our families, for their patience

CONTENTS

LIST OF TABLES

ACKNOWLEDGMENTS

The research that underlies this book has benefited from a number of individuals. First and foremost are our families, to whom this book is dedicated. As well, we especially wish to thank Gregory Tassey of the Program Office and Rosalie Ruegg of the Advanced Technology Program, both at the National Institute of Standards and Technology (NIST), for their resource support of the case studies presented herein. Also, there are the NIST laboratory directors and their support staff who provided invaluable background information throughout the research stages described herein. David Leech, Michael Marx, and Matthew Shedlick, all of TASC, participated in several of the case studies. We are delighted to acknowledge also their role as co-authors in the appropriate chapters of this book. Along with that attribution is the original citation of the NIST Planning Report prepared for the Program Office. The reader should be aware that the source of all data in such chapters is those reports. We also thank the industry scientists, engineers, and managers who generously participated with their time and knowledge in the survey portions of the case studies. Finally, a special thanks to Ranak Jasani, Acquisitions Editor in Economics, and Yana Lambert, Editorial Assistant, both of Kluwer Academic Publishers, for their thoughtful guidance throughout this project.

1 INTRODUCTION: WHY EVALUATE PUBLIC INSTITUTIONS

INTRODUCTION

Why should public institutions be evaluated? To answer such a basic question one should consider the broader issue of accountability, namely, should public institutions be accountable for their actions? If the answer is in the affirmative, and we believe that it is, then the question of how to evaluate a public institution—technology-based or otherwise—becomes relevant. This book focuses on the evaluation process in one public institution, the National Institute of Standards and Technology (NIST).

In the United States, the concept of *fiscal accountability* is rooted in the fundamental principles of representation of the people, by the people. However, as a more modern concept, accountability can be traced to the political reforms initiated by President Woodrow Wilson. In response to scandal-ridden state and local governments at the turn of the century, the concept of an impartial bureaucracy took hold in American government. Accountability, neutrality, and expertise became three of Wilson's reform themes. Shortly thereafter, Congress passed the Budget and Accounting Act of 1921, and that began the so-called modern tradition of fiscal accountability in public institutions.

Building on the general concept of accountability established in the more recent Competition in Contracting Act of 1984 and the Chief Financial Officers Act of 1990, the Government Performance and Results Act (GPRA) of 1993 was passed. The focus of GPRA is *performance accountability*; the purposes of the Act are to among other things improve the confidence of the American people in the capability of the federal government, initiate program performance reform, and improve federal program effectiveness and public accountability.

It is inevitable that managers in any public institution, technology-based or not, will become advocates for their own research agendas, and adherence to GPRA will only encourage this. Watching results on a day-to-day basis and witnessing the benefits of research and scientific inquiry to which one is committed understandably leads managers, and other participants in the research, to the intuitive conclusion that their activities are valuable. Regardless of the veracity of this conclusion, it may not be easily communicated to others, much less quantified in a meaningful way. Thus, when political and administrative superiors ask: "But how do you know your organization's research or technology-based investigation is effective?" managers often find themselves either dissembling or simply telling success stories. In this book, we show that a clear, more precise response to the question of performance accountability is possible through the systematic application of evaluation methods to document value.

OVERVIEW OF THE BOOK

Chapter 2, Public Policies Toward Public Accountability, overviews the legislative history of fiscal accountability beginning with the Budget and Accounting Act of 1921 and ending with the Government Performance and Results Act of 1993. GPRA is viewed as the centerpiece legislation that has most recently highlighted issues of public accountability. Such emphasis on public accountability has brought about a governmental agency-wide need for systematic guidelines applicable to, for our purposes, technology-based public institutions.

Chapter 3, Economic Models Applicable to Institutional Evaluation, discusses existing economic models and methods applicable for evaluating the performance of technology-based public institutions. The Griliches/Mansfield model is what we view as the traditional model. An alternative methodology for performance evaluation suitable for meeting the performance evaluation criteria outlined in GPRA is set forth. We call this methodology the counterfactual evaluation method, and we compare it to the Griliches/Mansfield approach.

Fundamental to any performance evaluation model are associated metrics that quantify the net social benefits associated with the performance activities of the technology-based public institution being studied. These metrics include, among others, the internal rate of return, the implied rate of return or adjusted internal rate of return, and the ratio of benefits-to-costs. Chapter 4, Performance Evaluation Metrics, discusses each of these evaluation metrics from a theoretical perspective and illustrates conceptually the applicability of each to the performance activities of a technology-based public institution.

The remainder of this book contains evaluation case studies conducted at NIST. Chapter 5, Case Studies: An Overview, summarizes the early technological history of NIST and the more recent evaluation history of its Program Office and of the Advanced Technology Program (ATP). Then, the organizational structure of this important federal laboratory is described. Finally, the case studies that are discussed in subsequent chapters are overviewed.

The case studies detailed in this book relate to a number of very different technologies, although the evaluation methodology applied is similar for each in that it is based on the counterfactual evaluation method.

Chapter 6 deals with NIST's optical detector calibration program. An optical detector is a device that measures, or responds, to optical radiation in the region of the electromagnetic spectrum roughly between microwaves and X-rays.

Chapter 7 considers an evaluation of NIST's thermocouple calibration program. A thermocouple is an electronic sensor for measuring temperature.

Chapter 8 focuses on the economic impacts of NIST's software error compensation research. Software error compensation is a computer-based mathematical technique for cost-effectively increasing the accuracy of coordinate measurement machines.

Ceramic phase diagrams are the focus of Chapter 9, and NIST's infrastructure investments in measurement technology associated with ceramic phase diagrams are discussed and evaluated from an economic perspective.

In Chapter 10 we discuss NIST's alternative refrigerant research program and the economic benefits to selected U.S. industries from that research. The chapter emphasizes the development of new types of refrigerants in response to environmental guidelines set forth in the Montreal Protocol in 1987.

Spectral irradiance standards are critical to industries concerned about luminous intensity. NIST's research and standards development in this area is evaluated in Chapter 11.

In Chapter 12, the first of two case studies specific to the evaluation efforts within the Advanced Technology Program is considered. This case study relates to the printed wiring board research joint venture funded by the ATP in 1991.

Then, in Chapter 13, a second ATP case study is considered. It relates to the flat panel display joint venture.

Finally, Chapter 14, Toward Best Practices in Performance Evaluation, sets forth best practices as gleaned from the evaluation experiences at NIST.

2 PUBLIC POLICIES TOWARD PUBLIC ACCOUNTABILITY

INTRODUCTION

The concept of public accountability can be traced to at least President Woodrow Wilson's reforms, and in particular to the Budget and Accounting Act of 1921. This Act of June 10, 1921, not only required the President to transmit to Congress a detailed budget on the first day of each regular session, but also it established the General Accounting Office (GAO) to settle and adjust all accounts of the government. We note this fiscal accountability origin because the GAO has had a significant role in the evolution of accountability-related legislation during the past decade.

The purpose of this chapter is to review the legislative history of legislation that falls broadly under the rubric of public accountability. As Collins (1997, p. 7) clearly notes:

> As public attention has increasingly focused on improving the performance and accountability of Federal programs, bipartisan efforts in Congress and the White House have produced new legislative mandates for management reform. These laws and the associated Administration and Congressional policies call for a multifaceted approach—including the provision of better financial and performance information for managers, Congress, and the public and the adoption of integrated processes for planning, management, and assessment of results.

Thus, the review in this chapter is intended to document the foundation upon which the National Institute of Standards and Technology (NIST) has developed its evaluation programs, and upon which other technology-based public institutions will be developing their own evaluation programs.

While students of political science and public administration will certainly point to subtleties that we have omitted in this review, our purpose is broader. Fundamental to any evaluation of a public institution is the recognition that the institution is accountable to the public, that is to taxpayers, for its activities. With regards to technology-based institutions, this accountability refers to being able to document and evaluate research performance using metrics that are meaningful to the institutions' stakeholders, meaning to the public.

The remainder of this chapter is divided into two major sections. The first section is concerned with performance accountability as reflected in the Chief Financial Officers Act of 1990 and in the Government Performance and Results Act of 1993. The second section builds on President Woodrow Wilson's concepts of fiscal accountability, referred to in Chapter 1, as reflected in the more recent Government Management Reform Act of 1994 and the Federal Financial Management Improvement Act of 1996. This chapter concludes with a summary of legislative themes related to public accountability.

PERFORMANCE ACCOUNTABILITY

Chief Financial Officers Act of 1990

The GAO has a long-standing interest and a well documented history of efforts to improve governmental agency management through performance measurement. For example, in February 1985, the GAO issued a report entitled "Managing the Cost of Government—Building An Effective Financial Management Structure" which emphasized the importance of systematically measuring performance as a key area to ensure a well-developed financial management structure.

On November 15, 1990, the 101st Congress passed the Chief Financial Officers Act of 1990. As stated in the legislation as background for this Act:

> The Federal Government is in great need of fundamental reform in financial management requirements and practices as financial management systems are obsolete and inefficient, and do not provide complete, consistent, reliable, and timely information.
>
> The stated purposes of the Act are:
>
> (1) Bring more effective general and financial management practices to the Federal Government through statutory provisions which would establish in the Office of Management and Budget a Deputy Director for Management, establish an Office of Federal Financial Management headed by a Controller, and designate a Chief Financial Officer in each executive department and in each major executive agency in the Federal Government.
> (2) Provide for improvement, in each agency of the Federal Government, of systems of accounting, financial management, and internal controls to assure the issuance of reliable financial information and to deter fraud, waste, and abuse of Government resources.

(3) Provide for the production of complete, reliable, timely, and consistent financial information for use by the executive branch of the Government and the Congress in the financing, management, and evaluation of Federal programs.

The key phrase in these stated purposes is in point (3) above, "evaluation of Federal programs." Toward this end, the Act calls for the establishment of agency Chief Financial Officers, where agency is defined to include each of the Federal Departments. And, the agency Chief Financial Officer shall, among other things, "develop and maintain an integrated agency accounting and financial management system, including financial reporting and internal controls," which, among other things, "provides for the systematic measurement of performance."

While the Act does outline the many fiscal responsibilities of agency Chief Financial Officers, and the associated auditing process, the Act's only clarification of "evaluation of Federal programs" is in the above phrase, "systematic measurement of performance." However, neither a definition of "performance" nor guidance on "systematic measurement" is provided in the Act. Still, these are the seeds for the growth of attention to performance accountability.

Government Performance and Results Act of 1993

Legislative history is clear that the Government Performance and Results Act (GPRA) of 1993 builds upon the February 1985 GAO report and the Chief Financial Officers Act of 1990. The 103rd Congress stated in the August 3, 1993, legislation that it finds, based on over a year of committee study, that:

(1) waste and inefficiency in Federal programs undermine the confidence of the American people in the Government and reduces the Federal Government's ability to address adequately vital public needs;
(2) Federal managers are seriously disadvantaged in their efforts to improve program efficiency and effectiveness, because of insufficient articulation of program goals and inadequate information on program performance; and
(3) congressional policymaking, spending decisions and program oversight are seriously handicapped by insufficient attention to program performance and results.

Accordingly, the purposes of GPRA are to:

(1) improve the confidence of the American people in the capability of the Federal Government, by systematically holding Federal agencies accountable for achieving program results;

(2) initiate program performance reform with a series of pilot projects in setting program goals, measuring program performance against those goals, and reporting publicly on their progress;
(3) improve Federal program effectiveness and public accountability by promoting a new focus on results, service quality, and customer satisfaction;
(4) help Federal managers improve service delivery, by requiring that they plan for meeting program objectives and by providing them with information about program results and service quality;
(5) improve congressional decisionmaking by providing more objective information on achieving statutory objectives, and on the relative effectiveness and efficiency of Federal programs and spending; and
(6) improve internal management of the Federal Government.

The Act requires that the head of each agency submit to the Director of the Office of Management and Budget (OMB):

> … no later than September 30, 1997 … a strategic plan for program activities. Such plan shall contain … a description of the program evaluations used in establishing or revising general goals and objectives, with a schedule for future program evaluations.

And, quite appropriately, the Act defines program evaluation to mean "an assessment, through objective measurement and systematic analysis, of the manner and extent to which Federal programs achieve intended objectives." In addition, each agency is required to:

> … prepare an annual performance plan [beginning with fiscal year 1999] covering each program activity set forth in the budget of such agency. Such plan shall … establish performance indicators to be used in measuring or assessing the relevant outputs, service levels, and outcomes of each program activity;

where "performance indicator means a particular value or characteristic used to measure output or outcome."

Cozzens (1995) correctly notes that one fear about GPRA is that it will encourage agencies to ignore what is difficult to measure, no matter how relevant. Alternatively, one could wear a more pessimistic hat and state that GPRA will encourage agencies to emphasize what is easy to measure, no matter how irrelevant.

FISCAL ACCOUNTABILITY

Legislation following GPRA emphasizes fiscal accountability more than performance accountability. While it is not our intent to suggest that performance accountability is more or less important than fiscal accountability, for we believe that both aspects of public accountability are important, the emphasis in the case studies conducted at NIST that are summarized in this book is on performance accountability. Nevertheless, our discussion would not be complete in this chapter without references to the Government Management Reform Act of 1994 and the Federal Financial Management Improvement Act of 1996.

Government Management Reform Act of 1994

The Government Management Reform Act of 1994 builds on the Chief Financial Officers Act of 1990. Its purpose is to improve the management of the federal government though reforms to the management of federal human resources and financial management. Motivating the Act is the belief that federal agencies must streamline their operations and must rationalize their resources to better match a growing demand on their services. Government, like the private sector, must adopt modern management methods, utilize meaningful program performance measures, increase workforce incentives without sacrificing accountability, and strengthen the overall delivery of services.

Federal Financial Management Improvement Act of 1996

The Federal Financial Management Improvement Act of 1996 follows from the belief that federal accounting standards have not been implemented uniformly through federal agencies. Accordingly, this Act establishes a uniform accounting reporting system in the federal government.

CONCLUSIONS

This overview of what we call public accountability legislation makes clear that government agencies are becoming more and more accountable for their fiscal and performance actions. And, these agencies are being required to a greater degree than ever before to account for their activities through a process of systematic measurement. For technology-based institutions in particular, internal difficulties are arising as organizations learn about this process.

As Tassey (forthcoming) notes, "Compliance ... is driving increased planning and impact assessment activity and is also stimulating greater attention to methodology." Perhaps there is no greater validation of this observation than the diversity of response being seen among public agencies, in general, and technology-based public institutions, in particular, as they grope toward an understanding of the process of documenting and assessing their public accountability. Activities in recent years have ranged from interagency discussion meetings to a reinvention of the assessment wheel, so to speak, in the National Science and Technology Council's (1996) report, "Assessing Fundamental Science."

We are of the opinion, having been involved in a number of such exercises and related agency case studies, that the performance evaluation program at NIST is at the forefront, as the methodology underlying the case studies summarized in this book illustrates.

3 ECONOMIC MODELS APPLICABLE TO INSTITUTIONAL EVALUATION

INTRODUCTION

The Government Performance and Results Act (GPRA) of 1993 provides a clear description of how public agencies, technology-based public institutions in particular, will be documenting themselves against implicit and explicit accountability criteria. They will, if they adhere to GPRA, be identifying outputs and quantifying the economic benefits of the outcomes associated with such outputs. The bottom line, except in rare instances, will be, in our opinion, a quantification of the benefits of the outcomes and then a comparison of quantified benefits to the public costs to achieve the benefits.

The methodology that is being employed and will likely be employed in the future can be simply described as follows:

Step 1: Quantify the technology-based investments of the institution or more likely a group within the institution,
Step 2: Identify the outputs associated with these investments,
Step 3: Identify the direct beneficiaries of the outcomes associated with the identified outputs, and
Step 4: Quantify the benefits received by the beneficiaries of the outcomes.

What could be more straightforward?

Implementation issues aside for the moment, this chapter focuses on Step 4. Step 1 through Step 3 will be illustrated through the case study summaries in this book. How does one, be it the institution itself or a third party studying the institution, quantify benefits?

The economic literature provides some guidance to the answer to this question. The Griliches/Mansfield approach to this issue is to quantify what we call spillover benefits, such as product improvements, process improvements, and the opening of new markets as a result of the public institution's research and subsequent outputs. Our alternative approach, and the approach that we believe is more applicable to an economic assessment of a technology-based public institution, is what we call the counterfactual evaluation model. And, it is this approach that has been adopted in large part at the National Institute of Standards and Technology (NIST) as the methodological foundation for its performance evaluation programs. Both approaches are discussed in this chapter.

COUNTERFACTUAL EVALUATION MODEL CONTRASTED WITH GRILICHES/MANSFIELD AND RELATED EVALUATION MODELS

Griliches (1958) and Mansfield et al. (1977) pioneered the application of fundamental economic insight to development of measurements of private and social rates of return to innovative investments. Streams of investment outlays through time—the costs—generate streams of economic surplus—the benefits—through time. Once identified and measured, these streams of costs and benefits are used to calculate rates of return and benefit-to-cost ratios.

In the Griliches/Mansfield models, the innovations evaluated can be conceptualized as causing a reduction in the cost of producing a good sold in a competitive market at constant unit cost. For any period, there is a demand curve for the good and a horizontal supply curve. Innovation lowers the unit cost of production, shifting downward the horizontal supply curve and thereby, at the new lower equilibrium price, resulting in greater consumer surplus (the economist's measure of value in excess of the price paid—the difference between the price consumers would have been willing to pay and the actual price, integrated over the amount purchased). Additionally, the Mansfield et al. formulation allows for producer surplus (measured as the difference between the price the producers receive and the actual marginal cost, integrated over the output sold, minus any fixed costs), collected as royalties by the owner of the intellectual property in the simplest competitive case.

The essential idea is that the social benefits are the streams of new consumer and producer surpluses generated, while the private benefits are the streams of producer surplus, not all of which are necessarily new because the surplus gained by one producer may be cannibalized from the pre-innovation surplus of another producer. Social and private costs will, in general, also be divergent.

A key feature of the Griliches/Mansfield applications is the focus on cost-reducing investments. That focus on "process innovation" results in a very clear way to estimate the gains in economic surplus. Although more difficult to do convincingly, the essential idea of weighing gains in economic surplus against investment outlays in order to calculate economically meaningful social and private rates of return can be extended to product innovations. The trick, of course, is in valuing the areas under new demand curves. Scherer (1979) and Trajtenberg (1990) provide pioneering work evaluating in different ways the returns to "product innovation." In principle, consumer value can be related to "hedonic" characteristics of products and thereby economists can measure the value of innovative investments that improve those characteristics.

The Griliches/Mansfield models and related ones, including those addressing product innovations that are not conceptualized as cost-lowering innovations, are used to calculate the economic rates of return for innovations. In this book, we do *not* calculate such rates of return. Instead we calculate counterfactual rates of return, and related benefit-to-cost ratios, that answer the question: Are public investments (for a technology being studied) more or less efficient than private investments? Thus, we do not calculate the stream of new economic surplus that is generated by an investment in technology; we instead take as given that stream of economic value and compare the counterfactual cost of generating the technology without public investment to the cost of generating the technology with such public investment. The benefits for our analyses are the additional costs that the private sector would have had to incur to get the same result as what occurred with the public investments. The stream of those benefits—the costs avoided by the private sector—are weighed against the public investments to determine our counterfactual rates of return and the related benefit-to-cost ratios. If the benefits exceed the costs (or equivalently, as discussed in Chapter 4, if the internal rate of return exceeds the opportunity cost of public funds), then the public has made a good or worthwhile investment. Public investment in the technology in such cases was more efficient than private investment would have been.

The Griliches/Mansfield and related models for calculating economic social rates of return add the public and the private investments through time to determine social investment costs, and then the stream of new economic surplus generated from those investments is the benefit. The analysis then can answer the question: What is the social rate of return to the innovation, and how does that compare to the private rate of return? We address a very different question, although we shall evaluate benefits (private-sector costs that are avoided because of the public sector's investments) and costs (the public sector's investments) using counterfactual rates of return and benefit-to-cost ratios. Holding constant the very stream of economic surplus that the Griliches/Mansfield and related models seek to measure, and making no attempt to measure that stream, we ask the counterfactual question, What would the private sector have had to invest in the absence of the public sector's investments? The answer gives the benefit of the public's investments, and we can calculate counterfactual rates of return and benefit-to-cost ratios that answer the key question for the evaluation of technology-based public institutions: Are the public investments a more efficient way of generating the technology than private sector investments would have been? In reality it may be impossible for the counterfactual private investment to replicate the streams of economic surplus generated by public investment. We address that point immediately below and then throughout the book.

Because of market failures stemming from the private sector's inability to appropriate returns to investments and from the riskiness of those investments, public funding may well be less costly than private investments that must be made in a contractual environment that tries to protect the private firms from opportunistic behavior that reduces the returns appropriated and increases the riskiness of the investments. In those cases where in fact our interactions with industry show that the market failures are so severe that the private sector could not have generated the same stream of economic surplus without the public investments, we cannot assume and hold constant the Griliches/Mansfield stream of economic surplus. In those cases, we estimate lower bounds on the additional value of products or the additional cost savings that occur because of the public's investments, and to get the benefits of the public investments, we add those lower-bound estimates of additional value to the additional investment costs that the private sector would have incurred in the absence of public investments.

A simple numerical example *in the context of a hypothetical public technology investment* will help focus the differences in the Griliches/Mansfield models and our own counterfactual model. In the Griliches/Mansfield models, the scenario would be as follows. A technology-based public institution invests $1 million in research. Directly traceable to that $1 million investment of public funds are identifiable technologies (outputs) that when adopted in the private sector lead to product improvements or process improvements (outcomes). The cumulative dollar benefits to the adopting companies or industries, producer surplus generated by reduced production costs, increased market share, or the like, represent the private benefits that have been realized from the public investment, and the new producer surplus and new consumer surplus generated represent the social benefits. A comparison of these social benefits and public costs leads to the determination of what is called a social rate of return. When using our counterfactual evaluation model, we do not attempt to measure *that* social rate of return to the investment in new technology. Instead, we ask whether the public investment achieved the new technology (and its associated return, whatever it may be) more efficiently than (counterfactual) private investment would have achieved the same result. As explained above, there may be cases of such severe market failure that the same result cannot be achieved with private investment, and we treat those cases by adding lower bound estimates of the lost value from inferior results to the counterfactual private investment costs. Thus, we do not calculate the social rate of return in the usual sense, although one could argue that we do calculate the *appropriate* social rate of return because only the subset of total benefits, from the technology, that we measure—namely the counterfactual costs avoided and the value of any extra performance enhancements generated by the public investments that the private sector could not generate—should be counted as the return to the public's investments.

Continuing with the discussion of the simple numerical example, consider again the technology-based public institution that invests $1 million in research. Outputs result from this research, and these outputs are used by identifiable beneficiaries in the private sector. The relevant counterfactual question that is addressed to these beneficiaries is: In the absence of these publicly-generated outputs and associated outcomes, what would your company have had to do to obtain the same level of technical capability that it currently has, and what resources over what time period would have been needed to pursue such an alternative. Because respondents to such a hypothetical question are comparing the institution's activities to those available in the market, and because they are aware of the market price of such services, the counterfactual evaluation model is, in a sense, a comparison of government costs to market prices. Importantly, the private costs of achieving the same level of technical capability in the counterfactual absence of public investments may include transaction costs that the public investments can avoid.

To illustrate with a simple example that sets the stage for the economic impact assessments that are summarized in later chapters, assume that the cumulative response from industry is that it would have to spend $200,000 a year in perpetuity to achieve the same level of results had the technology-based public institution not undertaken its research at a cost of $1 million. If the appropriate discount rate is 5 percent, then the private benefit-to-public cost ratio is 4-to-1. The present value of the benefits is $4 million (the capitalized value of $200,000 per year in perpetuity using a 5 percent discount rate or capitalization rate of 20); the cost is $1 million. Thus, in the absence of this institution's research activities, the cost of undertaking the research in the private sector would have been $4 million in discounted present value.

When the counterfactual evaluation model yields a benefit-to-cost ratio greater than 1.0, the implication is that the public research investment costs less than the private research investment needed to achieve the same results. Hence, a benefit-to-cost ratio greater than 1.0 implies that the rate of return on the public research investment is greater than the rate of return on the private research investment, had it been made. The research is thus worthwhile.

CONCLUSIONS

Table 3.1 compares the Griliches/Mansfield and related evaluation models with the counterfactual evaluation model. As seen from the table, the initial assumptions are distinct, and thus it is not surprising that the conceptual conclusions possible from each model are different. While we have not reviewed the academic and policy literature in this chapter in terms of applications of the more frequently used Griliches/Mansfield models, it is not an exaggeration to posit that their conceptual approach dominates the literature and likely is one of the first applications thought of when technology-based public institutions consider, from an economic perspective, a framework for analysis. That said, we are still of the opinion, based on the case studies that we have conducted at NIST as reported herein and as reported in Link (1996a, 1996b) and Link and Scott (1998b), that the counterfactual evaluation model is conceptually more appropriate for technology-based public institutions where there is a well defined set of beneficiaries or stakeholders for the emanating research.

Table 3.1. Comparison of the Griliches/Mansfield and Counterfactual Evaluation Models

	Griliches/Mansfield	Counterfactual
Assumptions	Cost-reducing innovation for a competitive market (or an estimable link from product characteristics to value of product innovations); the conventional paradigm of market demand and industry costs	Private sector investments could replace investments of the public sector
Data needed	Streams of public and private investment costs; streams of new consumer surplus and new producer surplus	Streams of public investment costs; counterfactual stream of private investment costs in the absence of the stream of public investments
Conceptual conclusions	Determination of the social and private rates of return to the investment in the technology	Determination of the relative efficiency of public versus private investment in the technology

4 PERFORMANCE EVALUATION METRICS

INTRODUCTION

It may well be the case that no topic is more intensely debated in the evaluation community than the topic of evaluation metrics. For every advocate of a particular metric there will be those who are equally critical. Why such a debate? The debate concerns substantive issues about the choice of appropriate discount rates and appropriate procedures for dealing with mathematical complexities, such as multiple rates of return, that can obscure economic interpretations. We have chosen to leave the debate outside the scope of our inquiry, and instead discuss three performance evaluation metrics used by the National Institute of Standards and Technology (NIST). NIST has "standardized" on three performance evaluation metrics, and those three metrics are discussed in this chapter: the internal rate of return, the implied rate of return or adjusted internal rate of return, and the ratio of benefits-to-costs. A fourth metric, net present value, is readily derived from the information developed for the benefit-to-cost ratio.

Each of these metrics is discussed here from a mathematical perspective. Our intent in this chapter is not to establish criteria by which to judge one metric over another, or to compare any of the three to a set of absolute criteria. Rather, our intent is simply to describe how each is calculated because all three of the metrics will be reported for many of the evaluation case studies in Chapters 6 through 13.

INTERNAL RATE OF RETURN

The internal rate of return (IRR) measure has long been used as an evaluation metric. By definition, the IRR is the value of the discount rate, i, that equates the present value (NPV) of a stream of net benefits associated with a research project (defined from the time that the research project began, $t = 0$, to a milestone terminal point, $t = n$) to zero. Net benefits refers to total benefits (B) less total costs (C) in each time period.

Mathematically,

(4.1) $$NPV = [(B_0 - C_0) / (1 + i)^0] + \ldots + [(B_n - C_n) / (1 + i)^n] = 0$$

where $(B_t - C_t)$ represents the net benefits associated with the project in year t, and n represents the number of time periods (years in most cases) being considered in the evaluation.

For unique, positive real solutions for i, from equation (4.1), the IRR can be compared to a value r that represents the opportunity cost of funds invested by the technology-based public institution. Thus, if the opportunity cost of funds is less than the internal rate of return, the project was worthwhile from an *ex post* social perspective.

Certainly, for a given research project, the calculated value of the internal rate of return is not independent of the time period over which the analysis is considered and it is not independent of the time path of costs and benefits. That is, for two projects, both with equal total costs and equal total benefits, the time path of the costs and of the benefits of each will dictate that the calculated internal rate of return for each will differ. Thus, projects should not be compared according to their calculated internal rate of return. The only benchmark to which the IRR can be compared in a meaningful way is to the opportunity cost of public funds. That said, how to measure the opportunity cost of public funds is not without dispute.

Given a theoretical opportunity cost of public funds or social discount rate, r, if r replaces i in equation (4.1), then when NPV equals zero, the ratio of benefits-to-costs equals 1.

Replacing i in equation (4.1) by r, and summing benefits and costs separately, it follows that:

(4.2) $$NPV = [\Sigma_{t=0 \text{ to } t=n} B_t / (1 + r)^t] - [\Sigma_{t=0 \text{ to } t=n} C_t / (1 + r)^t]$$

When NPV = 0 with reference to equation (4.2) then it follows that:

(4.3) $$\Sigma_{t=0 \text{ to } t=n} B_t / (1 + r)^t = \Sigma_{t=0 \text{ to } t=n} C_t / (1 + r)^t$$

or that the present discounted value of benefits equals the present discounted value of costs, or B/C = 1.

It is not uncommon for some policy makers, for example, to interpret an internal rate of return as an annual yield similar to that earned on, say a bank deposit. Such a direct comparison is, however, incorrect. The return earned on a bank deposit is a compounded rate of return. One invests, say $1,000 and earns interest on that $1,000 each year plus interest on the interest. That is not the case on an investment in a research project except in the abstract sense that for the internal rate of return a mathematical relation is computed *as if* the investment were in fact compounding. First, benefits do not necessarily compound, but more importantly, not all costs are incurred in the first time period and not all benefits are realized in the final time period.

IMPLIED RATE OF RETURN

While for most research projects public funding is lumpy, meaning that it occurs in uneven amounts over time, most private-sector benefits, resulting from public-sector investments, are also realized unevenly over time. For some projects, benefits are realized in a large amount shortly after the project is completed and then future benefits dissipate, and for other projects benefits are realized slowly after the research project is completed and then they increase rapidly. Whatever, some evaluators prefer to evaluate research projects using the implied rate of return or adjusted internal rate of return in an effort to overcome such timing effects (and others, such as multiple internal rates of return that can result when there are multiple reversals in the signs of net benefits through time) on an IRR calculation.

The calculation of this performance evaluation metric is based on the assumption that all public-sector research costs are incurred in the initial time period and all private-sector benefits are realized in the terminal time period. Albeit that this is rarely the case, the metric does have some interpretative value since in principle the project's stream of costs could be paid for with an initial investment at time zero sufficient to release the actual stream of costs, and since further in principle the benefits could be reinvested and realized with interest at the terminal time. The implied rate of return is the rate, x, that equates the value of all research costs discounted to the initial time period (present value of costs) to the value of all benefits inflated to the terminal period (terminal value of benefits) as:

$$(4.4) \qquad [\Sigma_{t=0 \text{ to } t=n} C_t / (1 + r)^t] (1 + x)^n = \Sigma_{t=0 \text{ to } t=n} B_t (1 + r)^{n-t}$$

Mathematically, the calculation of x is the nth root of the ratio of the terminal value of benefits (TVB) divided by the present value of costs (PVC), less 1:

$$(4.5) \qquad x = -1 + (TVB / PVC)^{1/n}$$

where,

$$TVB = \Sigma_{t=0 \text{ to } t=n} B_t (1 + r)^{n-t}$$

and,

$$PVC = \Sigma_{t=0 \text{ to } t=n} C_t / (1 + r)^t$$

However, the debatable aspect of this calculated metric is the value of r to use to discount all costs to the initial period and to inflate all benefits to the terminal period. Ideally, one would use for r those rates corresponding to the behavioral stories about financing with an initial period investment designed to release the flows of costs and about reinvesting benefits and realizing a terminal benefit.

Ruegg and Marshall (1990) advocate the use of the implied rate of return—although they prefer to call it the overall rate of return and others in the literature call it the adjusted internal rate of return—compared to the internal rate of return as a performance evaluation metric. They state that the chief advantage that the implied rate of return has over the internal rate of return is that it more accurately measures the rate of return that investors can expect over a designated period from an investment with multiple cash flows.

For comparative purposes, our implied rate of return, x, in equation (4.5) is mathematically equivalent to the Ruegg and Marshall overall rate of return, ORR. Equation (4.5) is equivalent to:

(4.6) $(1 + x)^n = TVB / PVC$

Ruegg and Marshall define the ORR as:

(4.7) $ORR = -1 + (1+r) (PVB / PVC)^{1/n}$

where (PVB / PVC) is the ratio of the present value of benefits (PVB) to the present value of costs, as:

(4.8) $PVB / PVC = [\Sigma_{t=0 \text{ to } t=n} B_t / (1 + r)^t] / [\Sigma_{t=0 \text{ to } t=n} C_t / (1 + r)^t]$

It follows from equation (4.7) that:

(4.9) $(ORR + 1)^n = (1 + r)^n (PVB / PVC)$

Our implied rate of return from equation (4.6) and the Ruegg and Marshall ORR from equation (4.9) are equivalent if:

(4.10) $TVB = (1 + r)^n PVB$

and clearly this is the case since:

(4.11) $(1 + r)^n PVB = (1 + r)^n \Sigma_{t=0 \text{ to } t=n} B_t / (1 + r)^t$

$= \Sigma_{t=0 \text{ to } t=n} B_t (1 + r)^{n-t}$

$= TVB$

as defined from equations (4.4) and (4.5).

RATIO OF BENEFITS-TO-COSTS

The ratio of benefits-to-costs is precisely that, the ratio of the present value of all measured benefits to the present value of all costs. Both benefits and costs are referenced to the initial time period, t = 0, as:

(4.12) $B / C = [\Sigma_{t=0 \text{ to } t=n} B_t / (1 + r)^t] / [\Sigma_{t=0 \text{ to } t=n} C_t / (1 + r)^t]$

A benefit-to-cost ratio of 1 implies that the project is a break-even project. Any project with B / C > 1 is a relatively successful project. Furthermore, the information developed to determine the benefit-to-cost ratio can be used to determine net present value (NPV = B - C) for each of several projects, allowing in principle one means of prioritizing projects *ex post.*

A policy planner might infer from a portfolio of NPV-prioritized completed projects a prioritization of potential new projects. While such inference would offer the policy planner a rationale for prioritizing potential new projects, caution should be exercised in this endeavor because the same degree of conservativeness in the estimation of net benefits may not have been used across the portfolio of completed projects.

CONCLUSIONS

While NIST certainly does not employ all of the metrics that are discussed in the literature (e.g., Bozeman and Melkers 1993, Kostoff 1998), the internal rate of return, the implied rate of return, and the ratio of benefits-to-costs are the standard performance evaluation metrics used.

Fundamental to the calculation of any of the above metrics is the availability of cost data and estimates of benefit data. Both of these issues are discussed conceptually in the following chapter with reference to the evaluation activities at NIST. Also, fundamental to implementing both the implied rate of return and the ratio of benefits-to-costs is a value for the discount rate, r.

One way to approximate r, the opportunity cost of public funds as described with reference to equation (4.2) and as used in equation (4.4), is to follow the guidelines set forth by the Office of Management and Budget (OMB) in Circular Number A-94. Therein it is stated that:

> Constant-dollar benefit-cost analyses of proposed investments and regulations should report net present value and other outcomes determined using a real discount rate of 7 percent.

Because the nominal rate, r, in equation (4.4) equals by definition the real rate of interest plus the rate of inflation, the practice at NIST is to approximate r when discounting costs as 7 percent plus the average annual rate of inflation from t = 0 to t = n (or, when data are forecasted, n is replaced with the last period for which the rate of inflation was actually observed) as measured by a Gross Domestic Product deflator. Certainly, the appropriate discount rate, the opportunity cost for the public funds, could differ for different public investments. We remain agnostic with regard to the "best" discount rate to apply to the particular investments of particular public technology institutions. As a practical choice grounded in the current thinking of the policy evaluation establishment, we shall follow throughout this book the recommendation of OMB; our conclusions are robust to sensible, moderate departures from that OMB-recommended discount rate.

5 CASE STUDIES: AN OVERVIEW

INTRODUCTION

This chapter sets the stage for the evaluation case studies that follow. As noted in the Acknowledgments, the evaluation case studies in this book were undertaken at the National Institute of Standards and Technology (NIST) as funded research projects. To set the stage for the case studies that follow, a brief history of NIST, based on the work of Cochrane (1966), is presented along with a description of the evolution of NIST's evaluation efforts of its research laboratories and of its Advanced Technology Program (ATP).

A BRIEF HISTORY OF NIST

The concept of the government's involvement in standards traces to the Articles of Confederation signed on July 9, 1778. In Article 9, § 4:

> The United States, in Congress assembled, shall also have the sole and exclusive right and power of regulating the alloy and value of coin struck by their own authority, or by that of the respective States; fixing the standard of weights and measures throughout the United States ...

This responsibility was reiterated in Article 1, § 8 of the Constitution of the United States:

> The Congress shall have power ... To coin money, regulate the value thereof, and of foreign coin, and fix the standard of weights and measures ...

In a Joint Resolution on June 14, 1836, that provided for the construction and distribution of weights and measures, it was decreed:

> That the Secretary of the Treasury be, and he hereby is directed to cause a complete set of all the weights and measures adopted as standards, and now either made or in the progress of manufacture for the use of the several custom-houses, and for other purposes, to be delivered to the Governor of each State in the Union, or such person as he may appoint, for the use of the States respectively, to the end that an uniform standard of weights and measures may be established throughout the United States.

On July 20, 1866, Congress and President Andrew Johnson authorized the use of the metric system in the United States. This was formalized in the Act of 28 July 1866—An Act to Authorize the Use of the Metric System of Weights and Measures:

> *Be it enacted* ..., That from and after the passage of this act it shall be lawful throughout the United States of America to employ the weights and measures of the metric system; and no contract or dealing, or pleading in any court, shall be deemed invalid or liable to objection because the weights or measures expressed or referred to therein are weights and measures of the metric system. ... *And be it further enacted*, That the tables in the schedule hereto annexed shall be recognized in the construction of contracts, and in all legal proceedings, as establishing, in terms of the weights and measures expressed therein in terms of the metric system; and said tables may be lawfully used for computing, determining, and expressing in customary weights and measures the weights and measures of the metric system ...

As background to this Act, the origins of the metric system can be traced to the research of Gabriel Mouton, a French vicar, in the late 1600s. His standard unit was based on the length of an arc of 1 minute of a great circle of the earth. Given the controversy of the day over this measurement, the National Assembly of France decreed on May 8, 1790, that the French Academy of Sciences along with the Royal Society of London deduce an invariable standard for all the measures and all the weights. Within a year, a standardized measurement plan was adopted based on terrestrial arcs, and the term mètre (meter), from the Greek metron meaning to measure, was assigned by the Academy of Sciences.

Because of the growing use of the metric system in scientific work rather than commercial activity, the French government held an international conference in 1872, which included the participation of the United States, to settle on procedures for the preparation of prototype metric standards. Then, on May 20, 1875, the United States participated in the Convention of the Meter in Paris and was one of the eighteen signatory nations to the Treaty of the Meter.

In a Joint Resolution before Congress on March 3, 1881, it was resolved that:

> The Secretary of the Treasury be, and he is hereby directed to cause a complete set of all the weights and measures adopted as standards to be delivered to the governor of each State in the Union, for the use of agricultural colleges in the States, respectively, which have received a

> grant of lands from the United States, and also one set of the same for the use of the Smithsonian Institution.

Then, the Act of 11 July 1890, gave authority to the Office of Construction of Standard Weights and Measures (or Office of Standard Weights and Measures), which had been established in 1836 within the Treasury's Coast and Geodetic Survey:

> For construction and verification of standard weights and measures, including metric standards, for the custom-houses, and other offices of the United States, and for the several States ...

The Act of 12 July 1894 established standard units of electrical measure:

> *Be it enacted ...*, That from and after the passage of this Act the legal units of electrical measure in the United States shall be as follows: ... That it shall be the duty of the National Academy of Sciences [established in 1863] to prescribe and publish, as soon as possible after the passage of this Act, such specifications of detail as shall be necessary for the practical application of the definitions of the ampere and volt hereinbefore given, and such specifications shall be the standard specifications herein mentioned.

Following from a long history of our nation's leaders calling for uniformity in science, traceable at least to the several formal proposals for a Department of Science in the early 1880s, and coupled with the growing inability of the Office of Weights and Measures to handle the explosion of arbitrary standards in all aspects of federal and state activity, it was inevitable that a standards laboratory would need to be established. The political force for this laboratory came in 1900 through Lyman Gage, then Secretary of the Treasury under President William McKinley. Gage's original plan was for the Office of Standard Weights and Measures to be recognized as a separate agency called the National Standardizing Bureau. This Bureau would maintain custody of standards, compare standards, construct standards, test standards, and resolve problems in connection with standards. Although Congress at that time wrestled with the level of funding for such a laboratory, its importance was not debated. Finally, the Act of 3 March 1901, also known as the Organic Act, established the National Bureau of Standards within the Department of the Treasury, where the Office of Standard Weights and Measures was administratively located:

> *Be it enacted by the Senate and House of Representatives of the United States of America in Congress assembled*, That the Office of Standard Weights and Measures shall hereafter be known as the National Bureau of Standards ... That the functions of the bureau shall consist in the custody of the standards; the comparison of the standards used in scientific investigations, engineering, manufacturing, commerce, and

> educational institutions with the standards adopted or recognized by the Government; the construction, when necessary, of standards, their multiples and subdivisions; the testing and calibration of standard measuring apparatus; the solution of problems which arise in connection with standards; the determination of physical constants and the properties of materials, when such data are of great importance to scientific or manufacturing interests and are not to be obtained of sufficient accuracy elsewhere.

The Act of 14 February 1903, established the Department of Commerce and Labor, and in that Act it was stated that:

> ... the National Bureau of Standards ..., be ... transferred from the Department of the Treasury to the Department of Commerce and Labor, and the same shall hereafter remain ...

Then, in 1913, when the Department of Labor was established as a separate entity, the Bureau was formally housed in the Department of Commerce.

In the post World War I years, the Bureau's research focused on assisting in the growth of industry. Research was conducted on ways to increase the operating efficiency of automobile and aircraft engines, electrical batteries, and gas appliances. Also, work was begun on improving methods for measuring electrical losses in response to public utility needs. This latter research was not independent of international efforts to establish electrical standards similar to those established over 50 years before for weights and measures.

After World War II, significant attention and resources were given to the activities of the Bureau. In particular, the Act of 21 July 1950 established standards for electrical and photometric measurements:

> *Be it enacted by the Senate and House of Representatives of the United States of America in Congress assembled,* That from and after the date this Act is approved, the legal units of electrical and photometric measurements in the United States of America shall be those defined and established as provided in the following sections. ... The unit of electrical resistance shall be the ohm ... The unit of electrical current shall be the ampere ... The unit of electromotive force and of electrical potential shall be the volt ... The unit of electrical quantity shall be the coulomb ... The unit of electrical capacity shall be the farad ... The unit of electrical inductance shall be the henry ... The unit of power shall be the watt ... The units of energy shall be the (a) joule ... and (b) the kilowatt-hour ...The unit of intensity shall be the candle ... The unit of flux light shall be the lumen ... It shall be the duty of the Secretary of Commerce to establish the values of the primary electric and photometric units in absolute measure, and the legal values for these units shall be those represented by, or derived from, national reference standards maintained by the Department of Commerce.

Then, as a part of the Act of 20 June 1956, the Bureau moved from Washington, D.C. to Gaithersburg, Maryland.

The responsibilities listed in the Act of 21 July 1950, and many others, were transferred to the National Institute of Standards and Technology when the National Bureau of Standards was renamed under the guidelines of the Omnibus Trade and Competitiveness Act of 1988:

> The National Institute of Standards and Technology [shall] enhance the competitiveness of American industry while maintaining its traditional function as lead national laboratory for providing the measurement, calibrations, and quality assurance techniques which underpin United States commerce, technological progress, improved product reliability and manufacturing processes, and public safety ... [and it shall] advance, through cooperative efforts among industries, universities, and government laboratories, promising research and development projects, which can be optimized by the private sector for commercial and industrial applications ... [More specifically, NIST is to] prepare, certify, and sell standard reference materials for use in ensuring the accuracy of chemical analyses and measurements of physical and other properties of materials ...

NIST's mission is to promote U.S. economic growth by working with industry to develop and apply technology, measurements, and standards. It carries out this mission through four major programs, the first two of which are discussed indirectly in the following two sections:

(1) Measurement and standards laboratories that provide technical leadership for vital components of the nation's technology infrastructure needed by U.S. industry to continually improve its products and services;
(2) A rigorously competitive Advanced Technology Program providing cost-shared awards to industry for development of high-risk, enabling technologies with broad economic potential;
(3) A grassroots Manufacturing Extension Partnership with a network of local centers offering technical and business assistance to smaller manufacturers; and
(4) A highly visible quality outreach program associated with the Malcolm Baldrige National Quality Award that recognizes continuous improvements in quality management by U.S. manufacturers and service companies.

EVALUATION ACTIVITIES OF THE PROGRAM OFFICE

The Program Office was established within NIST in 1968. Its mission is to support the Director and Deputy Director and to perform program and policy analyses; articulate and document NIST program plans; generate strategies, guidelines, and formats for long-range planning; analyze external trends, opportunities, and user needs regarding NIST priorities; coordinate, carry out, and issue studies; collect, organize, verify, and present descriptive NIST data; administer multi-organizational processes; provide staff support for key management committees; develop relevant budget documents; implement NIST information policies and standards; and perform economic impact analyses for NIST as a whole and produce analytical leadership for the laboratories' impact assessment efforts.

Following from the last of those stated missions, the Program Office initiated its first economic impact assessments as part of its overall mission and as part of an effort to establish the groundwork for future assessments. These forward looking demonstration projects were undertaken with the realization that NIST's laboratories should conduct economic impact assessments to enhance overall management effectiveness as well as to ensure public accountability and to document value (Link 1996a).

Recognizing the importance of effectively linking the complementary technology activity of government and industry, NIST as an agency began to address two fundamentally important questions. The first question is: How should NIST as an agency select where to invest public resources? The second question is: How should NIST measure the results of its investments in technology development and application?

Guidance on how NIST should answer the first question is beyond the scope of this book. However, we do note that part of an overall program evaluation should include a periodic fresh look at the reason that the government, rather than the private sector should be undertaking the investment(s) in question. As Link and Scott (1998a) have discussed, it is possible to demonstrate *a priori* aspects of market failure and thereby to justify on economic grounds particular investment strategies.

Toward formulating an answer to the second question, the Program Office is committed to conducting or supervising economic impact assessments within each of the seven research laboratories. As demonstration of NIST's overall commitment to this evaluation strategy, the cost of the evaluations is being born out of NIST's overall administrative budget rather than out of each laboratory's operating budget. Because of the relative newness of this activity, the Program Office, in consultation with individual laboratory directors, chose research areas that seemed, *a priori*, to have had measurable economic impacts on industry. This selective approach also has the advantage of developing in-house laboratory stakeholders in the genesis of a broader assessment plan.

The purpose of an economic impact assessment of a research project at NIST is to evaluate, both qualitatively and quantitatively, the benefits to industry that are associated with the research project and to compare those benefits, in a systematic manner, to the costs of conducting the research project. Industry is the focal benefactor based on NIST's mission as stated in the Omnibus Trade and Competitiveness Act of 1988: to "enhance the competitiveness of American industry ..." Certainly, industry is not the only sector of the economy that benefits from NIST's research. Economic impacts accrue to consumers and the public at large; however, potential users of research outputs within industrial sectors are of primary importance.

An economic impact assessment is different from other evaluation efforts that take place at NIST. For example, the directors of the NIST laboratories, listed below, regularly conduct or contribute to program evaluations. The purpose of these evaluations is to determine how well the portfolio of research projects within an industry- or technology-focused programmatic area aligns with the objectives of the program or laboratory; to understand how effectively the program is being managed; and to assess progress toward program and broader NIST objectives. Thus, a broad range of evaluation-based metrics are considered, including quantity and quality of technical work, intensity of interactions with constituents, level of satisfaction among constituent groups, variety and quantity of technical output, and some general indication of industry impacts.

In contrast, economic impact assessments focus on changes in financial and strategic variables within industrial organizations whose activities are directly affected by NIST research and associated services. Impact assessments are therefore narrower in scope than program evaluations, but in fact contribute to overall program evaluation. Economic impact assessments are generally conducted on completed or on-going projects that have been funded as a result of some prior project selection process. Such assessments are not intended to identify new research areas or to replace standard research project selection exercises, but they frequently contribute to program planning.

According to Tassey (forthcoming), NIST regularly undertakes economic impact assessments to estimate the contributions of its laboratory research to industrial competitiveness and to provide insights into the mechanisms by which such benefits are delivered to industry. Specifically:

> ... these studies are conducted to (1) provide planning-relevant information on the nature and magnitude of the economic impacts from NIST research projects, (2) convey to the policy and budget processes the rates of return to society from expenditures by NIST, and (3) provide data necessary to comply with Congressionally-mandated requirements (in particular, GPRA). ... In other words, economic impact assessments are functionally linked to both strategic planning studies [and economic policy rationales]. Together, the three comprise the basic elements of R&D policy analysis.

There was never the pretension that the research projects initially selected by the Program Office for assessment are representative of all research undertaken at NIST. But, it was the belief that over time a sufficient number of assessments would be undertaken so that there would be a distribution of quantifiable benefits from which to generalize about the economic impacts associated with NIST's collective activities, and hence to have some evidence relevant to the performance evaluation of NIST's measurement and standards laboratories.

The measurement and standards laboratories mission statement is:

> To promote the U.S. economy and public welfare, the Measurement and Standards Laboratories of the National Institute of Standards and Technology provide technical leadership for the Nation's measurement and standards infrastructure, and assure the availability of needed measurement capabilities.

The seven research laboratories at NIST, and their research missions are:

(1) Electronics and Electrical Engineering Laboratory (EEEL): The Electronics and Electrical Engineering Laboratory promotes U.S. economic growth by providing measurement capability of high impact focused primarily on the critical needs of the U.S. electronics and electrical industries, and their customers and suppliers.
(2) Chemical Science and Technology Laboratory (CSTL): The Chemical Science and Technology Laboratory provides chemical measurement infrastructure to enhance U.S. industry's productivity and competitiveness; assure equity in trade; and improve public health, safety, and environmental quality.
(3) Materials Science and Engineering Laboratory (MSEL): The Materials Science and Engineering Laboratory stimulates the more effective production and use of materials by working with materials suppliers and users to assure the development and implementation of the measurements and standards infrastructure for materials.
(4) Information Technology Laboratory (ITL): The Information Technology Laboratory works with industry, research, and government organizations to develop and demonstrate tests, test methods, reference data, proof of concept implementations, and other infrastructural technologies.
(5) Manufacturing Engineering Laboratory (MEL): The Manufacturing Engineering Laboratory performs research and development of measurements, standards, and infrastructure technology as related to manufacturing.
(6) Physics Laboratory: The Physics Laboratory supports U.S. industry by providing measurement services and research for electronic, optical, and radiation technologies.
(7) Building and Fire Research Laboratory: The Building and Fire Research Laboratory enhances the competitiveness of U.S. industry and public safety by developing performance prediction methods, measurement technologies, and technical advances needed to assure the life cycle quality and economy of constructed facilities.

The economic impact assessments at NIST are somewhat unique when compared to the evaluation activities in other government agencies in the United States and when compared to the evaluation activities in other countries. Regarding sister agencies, NIST, through the actions of the Program Office, is arguably at the forefront in terms of the evolution of a systematic methodology for conducting assessment studies as well as in terms of the actual number of completed assessment studies (Tassey forthcoming).

From an international comparative perspective, NIST also has some distinguishing characteristics. Of course, program evaluation is not unique to the United States, and certainly GPRA did not invent the wheel with respect to a need for a systematic approach to public accountability. Program evaluation has a long history, as carefully overviewed by Georghiou (1995). However, there are some notable and interesting dimensions that set the United States, in general, and NIST, in particular, apart. First, France is the only European country that joins the United States (through GPRA) to have a legislated mandate of institutionalized evaluation through its Comité National d'Evaluation de la Recherche. Ireland, the Netherlands, and the United Kingdom have what we call "cultural mandates," meaning that there are governmental expectations that evaluation will take place and these expectations have become part of the culture of agencies. For example, as Georghiou (1995, p. 6) notes:

> In the Netherlands, a desire in the centre of government (Parliament and Ministries) that evaluation should be performed is manifested only as an expectation that it should be done. This expectation is not accompanied by institutionalised processes and procedures; rather the implementation is left to the operators who form the intermediary level ...

Finally, it should also be noted that performance evaluation of outcomes is not the norm in the European countries. Rather, more common are *ex ante* peer reviews of projects and programs. Such evaluations generally are tied to funding allocations, or re-allocations; whereas at NIST there is a strong emphasis on using economic impact assessments to enhance management effectiveness.

EVALUATION ACTIVITIES OF THE ADVANCED TECHNOLOGY PROGRAM

The Advanced Technology Program (ATP) was established within NIST through the Omnibus Trade and Competitiveness Act of 1988, and modified by the American Technology Preeminence Act of 1991. The goals of the ATP, as stated in its enabling legislation, are to assist U.S. businesses in creating and applying the generic technology and results necessary to:

> Commercialize significant new scientific discoveries and technologies rapidly, and refine manufacturing technologies.

The ATP received its first appropriation from Congress in FY 1990. The program funds research, not product development. Most of the nearly 400 funded projects last from three to five years. Commercialization of the technology resulting from a project might overlap the research effort at a nascent level, but generally full translation of the technology into products and processes may take a number of additional years.

ATP was one of the first, if not the first, federal research programs to establish a general evaluation plan before the program had generated completed research projects, as emphasized by Link (1993). ATP's management realized early on that it would take years before social economic benefits associated with the program could be identified much less quantified. Nevertheless, management set forth an agenda for assembling and collecting relevant information. The operational aspects of the ATP evaluation plan contain both an evaluation of process and an evaluation of outcomes.

As stated by Ruegg (1998, p. 7):

> The ATP initiated evaluation at the outset of the program; first, to develop a management tool to make the program better meet its mission and operate more efficiently; and, second, to meet the many external requirements and requests for ATP program results. Demands for performance measures of the ATP are intense ... the ATP, like other federal programs, is subject to the evaluation requirements of the 1993 Government Performance and Results Act (GPRA).

Unlike the evaluation efforts of the Program Office, the results to date from ATP's evaluation efforts are not metric based. The reason is that the program is still, relative to the research programs of other technology-based public institutions, in its infancy and only in 1996 did the first funded project reach research completion. Thus, according to Ruegg (1998, p. 7):

> ATP has adopted a multicomponent evaluation strategy. Its main components include (1) descriptive (statistical) profiling of applicants, projects, participants, technologies, and target applications; (2) progress measures derived principally from surveys and ATP's "Business Reporting System;" (3) real-time monitoring of project developments by ATP's staff; (4) status reports on completed projects; (5) microeconomic and macroeconomic case studies of project impacts; (6) methodological research to improve the tools of longer term evaluation; (7) special-issues studies to inform program structure and evaluation; and (8) econometric and statistical analyses of the impacts of projects and focused programs.

CONCLUSIONS

Chapters 6 though 11 are economic impact assessment case studies conducted for the Program Office. These six case studies are summarized in Table 5.1. Of particular interest in the table is the output associated with each research project and the outcome of that research on industry (Tassey forthcoming).

There is not a common template for conducting and then communicating the findings from an economic impact assessment of laboratory projects. Each project considered has unique aspects that affect its assessment. However, all of the case studies have a quantitative aspect that relates, in a systematic manner, NIST research expenditures to the industry benefits associated with the outcomes noted in Table 5.1. In all cases, the counterfactual evaluation model was used to assess benefits.

The performance evaluation metrics discussed in Chapter 4 are calculated for each of these six research projects. We conclude for each that the metrics are sufficient to conclude "that the project was worthwhile." We do not, and we advise strongly against, comparing metrics across projects even within the same institution. Attempts to rank these or any projects *ex post* is likely to lead to spurious comparisons. As noted in Chapter 4, the numerical size of each metric is a function of the timing of benefits relative to costs and also the scope of benefits considered in the analysis.

Chapters 12 and 13 are evaluatory case studies conducted for ATP. As carefully stated by Ruegg above, the ATP evaluation program has a multi-faceted evaluation strategy. However, this strategy is only now beginning to be implemented because the earliest funded projects have just recently reached completion. Accordingly, the case study in Chapter 12 on the printed wiring board research joint venture and the case study in Chapter 13 on the flat panel display joint venture are distinct in the sense that the early-stage impacts differ. Also, these two case studies illustrate the difficulty in assessing economic impacts at a point in time when the underlying research has just been completed. Nevertheless, these are state-of-the-art ATP case studies, and in that regard they may act as a guide for other technology-based public institutions for their burgeoning research projects. Certainly, as the ATP's evaluation program matures to the point of that of the Program Office, and as funded projects reach completion and knowledge spills over into the private sector, ATP case studies will be more developed than the two presented here.

Table 5.1. Program Office-Sponsored Economic Impact Assessments

Chapter	Project	Output	Outcome
6	Optical detector calibration	Test method	Increased product quality Reduced transaction costs
7	Thermocouple calibration	Reference data	Increased product quality Reduced transaction costs
8	Software error compensation	Quality control algorithm	Increased R&D efficiency Increased productivity
9	Ceramic phase diagrams	Reference data	Increased R&D efficiency Increased productivity
10	Alternative refrigerants	Reference data	Increased R&D efficiency Increased productivity
11	Spectral irradiance standards	Test method	Reduced transaction costs

6 OPTICAL DETECTOR CALIBRATION PROGRAM

INTRODUCTION

An optical detector, either a photodetector or a thermal detector, is a device that generates a signal when light is incident upon it. A photodetector absorbs a photon of light and measures the electric current associated with the generated electrons. A thermal detector absorbs a photon of light, and as the temperature of the thermal detector increases the temperature change is measured.

During the 1970s, the use of photodetectors for radiometric purposes increased dramatically in response to improved reliability and decreased cost. In response, the National Institute of Standards and Technology (NIST), then the National Bureau of Standards (NBS), began in 1979 to modernize its detector calibration program. Since that time, the detector calibration program at NIST has expanded its effort and scope in order to meet the growing calibration needs of industry.

This case study quantifies the economic benefits to industry associated with NIST's calibration activities.

OPTICAL DETECTOR CALIBRATION

The Council for Optical Radiation Measurements (CORM) was formed as a non-profit organization in 1972 at a conference of industrial and governmental representatives interested in optical radiation measurements. Its stated aim is to establish a consensus among interested parties on industrial and academic requirements for physical standards, calibration services, and inter-laboratory collaboration programs in the field of optical radiation measurements. In 1979, motivated by the widespread availability and use of photodetectors for radiometric purposes during the 1970s, CORM recommended in its report on "Projected National Needs in Optical Radiation Measurements" that the then National Bureau of Standards (NBS) should provide detector spectral responsivity calibration services and such calibration services should be available for all modes of detector operations. In response, NBS developed a calibration package that could be rented by customers and used to transfer scales of detector responsivity. This package—the Photodiode Spectral Response Rental Package—served as the primary means of detector calibration until 1990.

In both 1982 and 1983, CORM again indicated a strong need for NBS to develop an in-house detector calibration program. While the rental program was servicing some of the needs of the optical community, the package was cumbersome and time consuming. It was finally decided at NBS that the organization should sell calibrated detectors that would provide consumers with scales of detector responsivity. Toward this end, a Detector Characterization Facility was created. It became operational in 1987. In 1990, NIST began selling detectors through its Special Test of Radiometric Detector program.

The Physics Laboratory, one of the seven research laboratories at NIST, is divided into six divisions, and the Optical Technology Division is one of the divisions. The Optical Technology Division meets the needs of the lighting, photographic, automotive, and xerographic industries, and government and scientific communities, by:

(1) Providing national measurement standards and services of optical technologies spanning the ultraviolet through microwave spectral regions for national needs in solar and environmental monitoring, health and safety, and defense;
(2) Developing and delivering measurement methods, standards, and data for: radiometry, photometry, spectroscopy, and spectrophotometry; and
(3) conducting basic, theoretical, and experimental research to improve services in optical and photochemical properties of materials, in radiometric and spectroscopic techniques and instrumentation, and in application of optical technologies.

The Optical Sensor Group, which maintains the Detector Characterization Facility, is one of five research groups within the Optical Technology Division. The Optical Sensor Group has responsibility for establishing the national measurement scale for the International System of units (SI) base unit, the candela; performing research and development on optical detectors for radiometry, photometry, colorimetry, and spectrophotometry, and providing measurement services for photodetector responsivity and photometry. These divisional and group responsibilities are an extension of the charge given to NBS under the Organic Act of 1901.

OPTICAL DETECTOR TECHNOLOGY

How Optical Detectors Work

As described by the Solar Energy Research Institute (1982) and by Saleh and Teich (1990), an optical detector is a device that measures, or responds, to optical radiation in the region of the electromagnetic spectrum roughly between microwaves and X-rays. On the electromagnetic spectrum this range is between 100 nm (nanometer) and 1,000 μm (micrometer). When a photon of light is incident on a photodetector, or transducer as it is often called, the detector responds with an electrical signal; on a thermal detector, the response is a temperature change.

A photodiode is a type of photodetector. More specifically, a photodiode is a photodetector that, based on semiconductor principles, transforms radiant energy or photons from a light source into a measurable electrical signal (e.g., voltage or current).

Activities of the Detector Characterization Facility

The majority of calibrations in the Detector Characterization Facility at NIST are specific to single-element photodiodes. Photodiodes are two-terminal (anode and cathode) semiconductor components with electrical characteristics that are designed to enhance their light sensitivity. They are used both to detect the presence of light and to measure light intensity. Most photodiodes consist of semiconductor material packaged with a window. When they are illuminated, a current is produced that is proportional to the amount of light falling on the photodiode.

The Detector Characterization Facility sells calibrated detectors sensitive to the ultraviolet, visible, and near infrared regions of the electromagnetic spectrum. The ultraviolet detectors sold by NIST are produced by UDT Sensors, Inc., and the visible and near infrared detectors currently sold are produced by Hamamatsu Photonics. The types of photodiodes calibrated, in terms of semiconductor materials used, are silicon, germanium, indium gallium arsenide, gallium phosphide, and silicon carbide.

While a customer could purchase a detector directly from one of these two manufacturers, or from others, the advantage of purchasing the detector from NIST is that is has been calibrated and thus is suitable for use as a secondary standard. Accordingly, along with the detector, the customer receives a calibration plot and a calibration table. The calibration plot depicts responsivity (i.e., current out (amps) per watts in) versus wavelength; the calibration table translates this information into tabular form. The calibration table lists the measured responsivities and their uncertainties for approximately 150 to 200 wavelengths in increments of 5 nm.

For a given wavelength, NIST calculates the power, in watts, of a given light source. The customer can thus use the calibrated photodetector and associated calibration table as a standard to certify the responsivity of the detectors that they use in their own production line or service.

Once an order is received at NIST, the customer will receive a calibrated detector and documentation within approximately six months. Depending on the type of detector, meaning the material from which the semiconductor is made and hence the portion of the spectrum to which it is applicable, the cost per calibration, including the detector, was in 1996 within the $1,500 to $2,300 range.

In addition to selling calibrated detectors, NIST also calibrates customer artifacts (detectors) and provides to each a calibration plot and table as described above. As with the use of the calibrated detectors, calibrated customer artifacts are then used as secondary standards.

U.S. OPTICAL DETECTOR INDUSTRY

There are no public data, or published trade data, on the competitive structure of the domestic photodiode industry. The data that are available from the U.S. Bureau of the Census are for the value of shipments of photodiodes in general. As shown in Table 6.1 for the seven-digit SIC product code 3674922—Photodiodes, the nominal value of shipments increased throughout the 1980s, and then there was a sizable jump between 1990 and 1991, reaching a peak in 1992 at $63.6 million. In real, inflation-adjusted dollars (not shown in the table), this industry grew steadily until 1992, and then softened.

In 1995—the latest data available when this study was being conducted in 1996—as shown in Table 6.1, the estimated size of the photodiode market was $52.9 million, with 16 non-captive producers. Domestically, the largest non-captive producers were UDT Sensors and EG&G Judson. The major domestic captive producers of photodiodes in that year were Texas Instruments, Honeywell, and Helwett-Packard.

Table 6.1. Value of Shipments for Photodiodes

Year	Value of Shipments ($millions)
1984	$11.3
1985	10.4
1986	14.8
1987	20.3
1988	39.0
1989	40.6
1990	40.5
1991	60.6
1992	63.6
1993	51.7
1994	49.7
1995	52.9

In a technologically-sophisticated industry such as photodiodes, the boundaries of the industry are drawn on the basis of the firms' capabilities to provide products that meet highly technical performance standards. Thus, based on discussions with industry experts, many of whom were interviewed for this case study, Table 6.2 represents an informed description of the structure of the domestic photodiode industry, based on 1995 value of shipments. Relatedly, Table 6.3 shows the major applications of photodiodes.

ECONOMIC IMPACT ASSESSMENT

Methodology for Collecting Benefit Data

For this study, management within the Physics Laboratory provided the name and contact person for 35 industrial customers from fiscal year 1991 to mid-1996. Military and university customers were excluded. This population was defined as the most informed group from which to collect information about industrial economic benefits attributable to NIST's detector calibration program and related services.

Table 6.2. Structure of the Domestic Photodiode Industry

Material Type	Share of the Market
Silicon (all types)	60%
Germanium	10
Indium gallium arsenide	20
Others	10

Each identified contact person was interviewed by telephone. However, the final sample of customers from whom benefit data were collected is less than the population of 35 customers. There are two reasons for this reduction. One reason is that some listed contact persons were from a procurement office within the company that purchased the detector and thus were not knowledgeable about issues to be discussed; when possible, referrals were pursued. The other reason is that some contact persons were no longer with the company, and rarely in such cases could an alternative contact person be identified. The final sample of customers totaled 23.

By so defining the sample of customers from which qualitative and quantitative information would be collected, the study is confined to considering only a subset of the beneficiaries of first-level economic benefits, that is those benefits accruing to customers who directly interact with NIST's calibration facility, as opposed to total social benefits, that is those benefits accruing to society in general such as to those who purchase the more accurate instruments that contain calibrated detectors. Thus, the performance evaluation metrics calculated in this case study are lower-bound estimates of the total economic benefits that society receives from NIST's expenditures of public moneys. Not all first-level benefits are estimated, and certainly, if second-level benefits were considered, the magnitude of the total benefits associated with NIST's calibration activities would increase. Recalling the explanation of the counterfactual method in Chapter 3, the second-level benefits would include the loss in product value or in cost reduction resulting if the first-level beneficiaries were unable to replace the lost NIST technology completely with their own counterfactual investments. If the first-level beneficiaries were able to replace NIST's technology completely with their counterfactual investments, then there would be no further second-level benefits to add (ignoring any net surplus changes because prices may change to reflect the new private investment costs).

Table 6.3. Application Areas for Photodiodes

Spectral Region	Photodiode Product	Major Application
Vacuum ultraviolet	Silicon photodiodes	Industrial and scientific measurement instruments; space, atmospheric, defense, and environmental applications
Ultraviolet	UV enhanced photodiodes and gallium arsenide photodiodes	Pollution and other types of optical sensors; spectrophotometers; medical instruments; UV detectors; lighting; colorimeters; space, atmospheric, defense, and environmental applications
Visible	Silicon photodiodes, gallium arsenide photodiodes, and cadmium sulfide cells	Pollution and other types of optical sensors; color and appearance; lighting; many forms of transportation signals; electronic displays; exposure meters; photography; auto-strobe and auto-focus illuminators; medical instruments; flame monitors; light-sensing process control; space, atmospheric, defense, and environmental applications
Near infrared	Silicon, germanium, and indium gallium arsenide photodiodes	Optical communications; night vision and photography; range finders; computers; automatic control systems; home appliances; medical instruments; laser monitors, radiation thermometers; space, atmospheric, defense, and environmental applications

As shown in Table 6.4, the 23 surveyed respondents represented three broadly-defined industrial sectors: aerospace and defense, lighting equipment, and scientific instrumentation. The scientific instrumentation sector contains the two leading domestic detector manufacturers and other detector assemblers. In all cases, discussions took place with a scientist who not only had interacted in the past with NIST's calibration facility but also was intimately familiar with the uses of the calibrated detector within their company.

Table 6.4. Distribution of Optical Detector Survey Respondents

Industrial Sector	Respondents
Aerospace and defense	2
Lighting equipment	5
Scientific instruments	16

Survey Findings

After discussions about the nature of the company's uses of the calibrated detectors—and each respondent reported that their NIST-calibrated detector was used as their company's primary standard—each surveyed individual was asked a counterfâctual question: In the absence of NIST's calibration facility and services, what would your company do to ensure measurement accuracy? Selected qualitative responses to this question are reported in Table 6.5; some individuals offered more than one response.

Table 6.5. Qualitative Responses to the Counterfactual Optical Detector Survey Question

Responses	Frequency
Rely on foreign national laboratories	17
Manually characterize detectors	4
Build own laboratory	3
Have no idea	3
Likely go out of business	1

More specific than the qualitative responses in Table 6.5 to the counterfactual question are the following paraphrases or direct quotations:

(1) "We'd use NRC [National Research Council] in Canada or the national laboratory in the U.K. We've had some experience with both of them and they are less expensive than NIST but NIST is state-of-the-art."

(2) "It is a terrifying thought to think about dealing with foreign labs over which we have no ability for input; the red tape is overwhelming."
(3) My company would have three options: (i) create our own internal detector standard, (ii) rely on NRC in Canada, deal with the red tape and accept greater uncertainty, or (iii) rely on private sector calibration companies and accept greater uncertainty.
(4) "We would build our own laboratory because we cannot compromise on accuracy."
(5) "We would build our own lab in the absence of NIST, and we may do that anyway because NIST is too slow."
(6) We would manually maintain an internal baseline.

In many instances, those interviewed made qualitative observations about NIST's calibration program. The following remarks are representative:

(1) "The real loss is that no foreign laboratory can duplicate NIST's frontier research."
(2) "Of all the things I have to do in my job, the most enjoyable is working with the people at NIST."
(3) "NIST traceability gives us legitimacy in the marketplace."

It was apparent from the interviews that industry views the calibration services at NIST as a cost reducing infrastructure technology that increases product quality. Alternatives do exist to NIST's services, although the use of these alternatives includes an economic cost characterized in terms of greater measurement uncertainty and greater transactions cost.

Every individual interviewed responded to the counterfactual survey question, even if in a nebulous way. Most of the individuals interviewed were able to quantify their responses to the counterfactual question in terms of either additional person-months of effort that would be needed to pursue their most likely alternative, that is additional person-months of effort needed to deal with the red tape associated with foreign laboratories, or in terms of additional direct labor or capital expenditures. Five of the 23 respondents were simply unable to quantify the additional costs that they had qualitatively described.

Representative responses are:

(1) "Absent NIST we would manually characterize our detectors, but we'd need an extra man-year of effort per year to do so."
(2) "Without NIST we would need at least one full-time scientist to obtain and maintain a base line for us, and to gain back consumer confidence."
(3) "Our main probable action would be to create an internal detector standard, at an annual cost of between $30,000 and $40,000."
(4) We have had experience with the U.K. lab. They are slow but the quality is about the same as NIST. However, the red tape in dealing with them makes me think that if we did it on a regular basis it would cost us one-half a man-month each year forever.

(5) "While we could get by and adjust to the red tape associated with the labs in the U.K., the real loss would be in research; NIST is the catalyst and prime mover in world research on accuracy. For us to pick up the slack, it would cost us at least one-half of a man-year per year for a new scientist."

Quantifying Economic Benefits

For the eighteen (of 23) companies interviewed that were able to quantify additional costs to pursue their stated alternatives absent NIST's calibration services, the total annual cost, that is the sum of the additional costs to each of the eighteen companies, is $486,100. This total is based on additional information obtained from each respondent on the cost of a fully-burdened person-year. The mean and median response to the latter question was about $135,000. Certainly, the total from these eighteen individuals does not represent the total cost to all companies that interact with NIST for calibration services. However, in the absence of detailed information about the representativeness of this sample, it is assumed for the purpose of the case study that $486,100 represents the lower limit of annual first-level benefits to industrial customers. These expressed benefits, or annual cost savings, averaged $27,000 per surveyed company, or to generalize about 2.4 person-months of additional effort to overcome the transactions cost associated with dealing with a foreign laboratory or to maintain internal precision and accuracy.

NIST Research Costs

Table 6.6 shows the NIST costs to maintain and operate the detector calibration facility. There were no capital expenditures in 1995. Between 1994 and 1995, NIST lowered the overhead rate to its laboratories, thus explaining the decrease in the category labor costs plus overhead, although labor person-hours remained about the same. Between 1993 and 1994, however, NIST labor plus overhead costs increased about 6 percent. It is assumed, based also on discussions with those in the Physics Laboratory, for the purpose of forecasting from 1996 to 2001, discussed below, that costs will increase at 6 percent per year. These forecasted costs are also shown in Table 6.6.

Industrial Benefits

The interview discussions led to the conclusion that the annual cost savings associated with the availability of NIST's services was $486,100. While this estimate is the sum of cost-savings estimates from only eighteen companies that have had direct contact with NIST between 1991 and 1996, it is viewed here as the best conservative, lower-bound estimate available to approximate the total annual cost savings to all industrial companies that rely on NIST's optical calibration services.

Table 6.6. NIST Costs Associated with the Optical Detector Calibration Program

Fiscal Year	NIST Share of Capital Costs	Labor Costs Plus Overhead	Detector Calibration Revenue
1987	$30,000	$ 55,600	$ 3,415
1988	30,000	62,400	15,574
1989	30,000	71,900	19,608
1990	70,000	103,700	16,301
1991	70,000	117,400	63,708
1992	40,000	126,900	70,315
1993	40,000	135,200	79,469
1994	40,000	140,800	81,874
1995	0	129,400	78,706
1996	45,000	137,200	59,331
1997	47,700	145,432	
1998	50,562	154,158	
1999	53,596	163,407	
2000	56,812	173,211	
2001	60,221	183,604	

Annual data presented in Table 6.1 on the value of shipments of photodiodes reveals that the average annual rate of increase in the value of shipments since 1987 through 1995 was 20.1 percent. This percentage is used to forecast benefits from 1996 though 2001 under the assumption that industrial economic industrial benefits will increase in proportion to photodiode sales. Similarly, industrial benefits were estimated for previous years using the same percentage rate of decrease. Since the facility began in 1987, it is assumed that $0 benefits accrued to industry in that year.

The year 2001 was used to truncate the benefit and hence cost forecasts because, based on information from those in the Physics Laboratory, the average cycle of research in calibrations lasts for about five years. Also, it was the impression of those in industry that their cost saving estimates under the counterfactual scenario was reasonable for five years.

Table 6.7 reproduces actual and forecasted NIST costs from Table 6.6 and includes the industrial benefit forecasts just described. Note that the detector revenues are not subtracted from NIST's costs. We want to measure the social cost of NIST's investments, and that cost is the same whether or not the private sector pays a part of the costs. Of course, it would make sense to subtract the revenues if we were asking a narrower question about NIST's rate of return, but to answer the larger social question about the efficiency of developing the technology in the public laboratories versus without those laboratories, we must add all of the additional investment costs for a given scenario. The fact that the private sector is willing to pay for detector services reflects the value obtained from the NIST technology, but we want to know the costs for the scenario with NIST and the cost for the counterfactual scenario without NIST (and any lost value because the counterfactual costs do not completely replicate the results of NIST's investments).

Performance Evaluation Metrics

Finally, Table 6.8 summarizes the value of the three NIST performance evaluation metrics, discussed in Chapter 4, using a discount rate equal to 7 percent plus the average annual rate of inflation from 1987 through 1995; 3.69 percent. Certainly, on the basis of these metrics, the Optical Detector Calibration Program is worthwhile.

CONCLUSIONS

NIST responded to the increasing use of photodetectors in industry during the 1970s, and the associated need for calibration services, by modernizing its detector calibration program in 1979. Since that time, the program has expanded its efforts and scope in order to meet the growing calibration needs of the industrial community; in particular, NIST's Detector Characterization Facility began operations in 1987.

The findings from this economic impact assessment are very conservative in terms of the underlying assumptions used to generate past and future industrial benefits, and the findings clearly show that NIST, through the Detector Characterization Facility within the Physics Laboratory, is serving industry well.

Table 6.7. Actual and Forecasted NIST Costs and Forecasted Industrial Benefits for the Optical Detector Calibration Program

Fiscal Year	NIST Costs	Industrial Benefits
1987	$ 85,600	$ 0
1988	92,400	112,300
1989	101,900	134,873
1990	173,700	161,982
1991	187,400	194,541
1992	166,900	233,643
1993	175,200	280,606
1994	180,800	337,008
1995	129,400	404,746
1996	182,200	486,100
1997	193,132	583,806
1998	204,720	701,151
1999	217,003	842,083
2000	230,023	1,011,341
2001	243,825	1,214,621

Table 6.8. Performance Evaluation Metrics for the Optical Detector Calibration Program

Performance Evaluation Metric	Estimate (rounded)
Internal rate of return	53%
Implied rate of return	17%
Ratio of benefits-to-costs	2

There are potentially multiple real, positive solutions to the internal rate of return problem when solved in the customary way. In 1990, costs exceed benefits, and as a result there is an additional negative net cash flow beyond the initial one between 1987 and 1988. The equation from which the internal rate of return is computed is a nth-order polynomial where n is the number of years with cash flows beyond the initial outflow. The number of roots for the polynomial will be n, which for the case here is 14. Most of these roots are imaginary. The actual number of real, positive rates of return will be at most equal the number of reversals in sign for the net cash flows, but will also depend on the magnitude of the net cash flows and need not be as great as the number of reversals in sign for the net cash flows. Typically, all the net cash flows are positive after the initial negative outflow; and therefore, typically there is at most one real, positive rate of return. Despite the extra reversals in sign in this case, there is still only one real, positive solution, namely 0.527314, rounded to 53 percent in Table 6.8.

We observed in Chapter 4 that Ruegg and Marshall offer a convenient way to handle the cases with multiple rates of return. The implied rate of return provides a meaningful rate of return in such cases and that is one of the reasons, in addition to its behavioral and intuitive appeal discussed in Chapter 4, that we present it throughout this book. It is just one of a class of sensible solutions, however. In the present case, in 1990 there were costs of \$173,700 and benefits of \$161,982. To convert such a negative net cash flow to a positive one, we can reconfigure the problem in several different ways. For one example, the government could invest an additional (\$173,700 / $(1+r)^3$) in 1987, where r is the rate at which it can earn interest on its investment, and pledge the proceeds of that investment to meet the project's liabilities in 1990. The net cash flows for the project now show an additional outflow of (\$173,700 / $(1+r)^3$) in 1987, but in 1990, the net cash flow is simply the positive inflow of \$161,982, and the set of net cash flows shows the typical single reversal in sign. If, for example, r equals 0.10, then to the project's initial cost in 1987 we would add \$130,503, and the benefits for 1990 would be \$161,982 while the costs would now be zero (they were paid for with an additional initial investment in 1987 of \$130,503 that was sufficient to cover the costs of \$173,700 that occurred in 1990). The project's set of net cash flows now conforms to the typical project with one sign reversal. The internal rate of return for the reconfigured net cash flows is 41 percent (rounded). Such a simple reconfiguration of the stream of net cash flows can be used to avoid the multiple rate of return problem.

7 THERMOCOUPLE CALIBRATION PROGRAM*

INTRODUCTION

The thermocouple calibration program at the National Institute of Standards and Technology (NIST) resides within the Chemical Science and Technology Laboratory (CSTL). As discussed in Chapter 5, CSTL is one of seven research laboratories at NIST. CSTL's mission is to provide the chemical measurement infrastructure for enhancing the productivity and competitiveness of U.S. industry, assuring equity in trade, and improving public health, safety, and environmental quality. Such measurement technology is germane to industrial research and development, product application, improvements in the design and manufacturing of quality products, proof of performance, and marketplace transactions that include the successful entry of U.S. products into international markets.

Thermocouple calibration allows accurate measuring of temperature, and NIST's role as the lead U.S. agency for temperature measurement is to overcome technical and business barriers that require an impartial position, expertise in a wide range of measurement areas, direct access to complementary national standards, and the motivation to deliver the technical infrastructure to a wide range of supplier and user industries.

All temperature measurements must ultimately trace back to a national standard to provide consistency and accuracy across disparate organizations and industries. NIST has the legal mandate in the United States for providing the national standards that form the fundamental basis for all temperature measurements made in domestic industries, as previously discussed. Realizing and maintaining national temperature standards in terms of the scientific first principles and the constants of nature that define the International Temperature Scale is difficult technically and requires a dedicated laboratory capability. The CSTL develops and maintains the scientific competencies and laboratory facilities necessary to preserve

* This chapter was co-authored with Michael L. Marx. See Marx, Link, and Scott (1997).

and continuously refine the basic physical quantities that constitute the national temperature standard. Further, NIST has a mandate to apply these basic measurement standards to develop uniform and widespread measurement methods, techniques, and data.

THERMOCOUPLES : A TECHNICAL OVERVIEW

Thermocouple Circuits

A thermocouple is an electronic sensor for measuring temperature. Thermocouples operate according to the Seebeck Effect, wherein a closed circuit formed by two dissimilar wires (thermoelements) produces an electrical voltage when a temperature difference exists between the contact points (junctions). The electrical potential difference that is produced is called the thermoelectric electromotive force (emf), also known as the voltage output of the thermocouple. The Seebeck Effect occurs because of the difference in the energy distribution of thermally energized electrons in the material compositions of each thermoelement. The fact that thermoelectric emfs vary from metal to metal for the same temperature gradients allows the use of thermocouples for the measurement of temperature (Burns and Scroger 1989, Burns 1993).

Thermocouple Types

Approximately 300 combinations of pure metals and alloys have been identified and studied as thermocouples. Such a broad selection of different conductors is needed for applications requiring certain temperature ranges as well as for protection against various forms of chemical contamination and mechanical damage. Yet, only a few types having the most desirable characteristics are in general use.

The eight most common thermocouple types used in industry are identified by letters: base-metal types E, J, K, N, and T; and noble-metal types B, R, and S. The letter designations were originally introduced by the Instrument Society of America (ISA) to identify certain common types without using proprietary trade names, and they were adopted in 1964 as American National Standards. The letter-types are often associated with certain material compositions of the thermocouple wires. However, the letter-types actually identify standard reference tables that can be applied to any thermocouple having an emf versus temperature relationship agreeing within the tolerances specified in the table, irrespective of the composition of the thermocouple materials. The letter-type thermocouples comprise about 99 percent of the total number of thermocouples bought and sold in commerce.

Thermocouples made from noble-metal materials, such as platinum and rhodium, are significantly more expensive than those made from base-metal materials, such as copper and iron. For example, the 1996 prices for 0.015 inch diameter bare wires made of various platinum-rhodium alloys range from $25 to

$101 per foot, while the price range of similar base-metal wire is $0.20 to $0.24 per foot.

Thermocouple Calibration

Thermocouples must be calibrated for accurate temperature determination. In most cases, calibration involves measuring the thermoelectric emf of the thermocouple under evaluation as a function of temperature. The latter is determined by a reference thermocouple.

The calibration process generally consists of three steps. In the first step thermoelectric emf values of the thermocouple are measured either at a series of approximately uniform intervals of temperature or at certain fixed points. In the second step, appropriate mathematical methods are used to fit the difference between the measured emf values and those of a reference temperature. And in the third step, emfs as a function of temperature are expressed in both a calibration table and their given mathematical relationship.

The reference functions and tables used in calibrations of standard letter-type thermocouples must relate to a specified temperature scale. International agreements have been in place since 1927 on scales of temperature for scientific and industrial purposes. Updated about once every 20 years, the scale now in use is the International Temperature Scale of 1990 (ITS-90). ITS-90 was adopted during the 1989 meeting of the International Committee of Weights and Measures.

The extent of thermocouple calibration for practical temperature measurement depends mainly on the accuracy and stability required for the particular application. Stability refers to the ability of a thermocouple to achieve repeatable temperature versus emf characteristics with successive temperature measurements. An unstable thermocouple can go out of calibration or drift, which is a serious fault because of the resulting incorrect reading of temperature.

Wire suppliers typically perform sample calibrations on short wire lengths from spools containing up to 1,000 feet of wire. Sample calibrations of base-metal wire provide tolerances generally ranging from ± 0.25 percent to ± 0.75 percent of the temperature versus emf values in the standard reference tables, which provides sufficient accuracy for a wide variety of technical work. Certain suppliers of noble-metal wire claim to provide even tighter tolerances, ranging from ± 0.10 percent to ± 0.33 percent. However, uncertainties in process control and the need for more accurate measurements demand additional calibrations by certain suppliers and users of thermocouples. For example, the stringent accuracy and stability demands for temperature measurement made in semiconductor manufacturing processes often require calibration of every thermocouple.

Significant differences in stability and accuracy exist between the noble-metal and the base-metal types of thermocouples. Noble-metal type thermocouples tend to have fairly stable calibrations and tight calibration tolerances. The base-metal types are less stable, that is more likely to go out of calibration with frequent use, and have larger tolerances. Therefore, the more stringent the stability and accuracy requirements of the particular application, the more likely that users pay the higher costs for noble-metal thermocouples.

THERMOCOUPLES: AN INDUSTRIAL OVERVIEW

Thermocouple Applications

The thermocouple is the oldest and the most widely used electronic temperature sensing device. Other devices, such as thermistors, resistance temperature detectors, and integrated circuit sensors, can be substituted for thermocouples, but only over a limited temperature range. Therein lies the primary advantage of thermocouples, their use over a wide temperature range (-270 °C to 2,100 °C). Other key advantages are that thermocouples provide a fast response and are unaffected by vibration. They are also self-powered, versatile, inexpensive, and simple in their construction. The calibration of a thermocouple is, however, affected by material inhomogeneity (i.e., nonuniformity of physical composition) and contamination, and their operation is susceptible to electrical interference.

Thermocouples are used in a wide variety of applications, ranging from medical procedures to automated manufacturing processes. Whenever temperature is an important parameter in a measurement or in a control system, a thermocouple will be present. Their use in engineering applications, for example, has been increasing because thermocouples like other types of electronic measurement sensors are compatible with microprocessor instrumentation.

Table 7.1 characterizes levels of uncertainty for a variety of products and manufacturing processes that use thermocouples for temperature measurement from most stringent to least stringent. NIST uses the term uncertainty as the quantitative measure of inaccuracy. Applications having the most stringent requirements of uncertainty have greater needs for calibration knowledge than those applications having the least stringent requirements.

Certain industries have applications that are very sensitive to temperature change. According to various industry representatives, the four industries having the most stringent accuracy and stability requirements for temperature measurement are food, beverage, and drugs; semiconductor manufacturing; military and aerospace; and power utilities. For example, small temperature measurement inaccuracies in burning fuel for generating electrical power can translate into large inefficiencies and hence large costs.

A utility industry representative stated as part of this case study's background research that an inaccuracy of 1 °C would result in an annual $100,000 loss in pretax profits for a single fossil-fuel power generation plant. Also, IBM reported that a 3 °C miscalculation in a sintering process can jeopardize a furnace load of substrates worth in the millions of dollars. Additionally, a supplier of gas turbines used in aircraft stated that if the on-board temperature measurements of thermocouples used in the turbine are inaccurate by 1 °C, then the aircraft would burn 2 percent more fuel. Therefore, such thermocouple users with high accuracy requirements have greater economic sensitivity than the majority of users.

Table 7.1. Sample Applications of Thermocouples by Common Requirements of Uncertainty

Thermocouple Application
Most Stringent
Drug testing
Pharmaceutical chemical manufacturing
Moisture measurement in grain
Rapid thermal processing in semiconductor manufacturing
Glass softening point and forming
Steam turbine operation for electrical utilities
Moderately Stringent
Aircraft turbine engine operation
Residential thermostat
Metal sintering
Glass container formation
Tire molding
Least Stringent
Glass annealing
Metal heat-treating
Plastic injection molding
Residential stove operation
Steel production furnace

Cost and Quality Drivers for Accuracy

According to thermocouple experts, the key factors in obtaining accurate measurements in thermocouple thermometry are:

(1) Quality of the components in the temperature measurement system,
(2) Minimizing contamination in thermocouple wires, and
(3) Quality of calibration data that are traceable to standards at NIST.

In addition to absolute accuracy, the consistency of a temperature measurement in a fixed environment, such as a furnace, that requires periodic replacement of thermocouples is also critical in maintaining process control. Therefore, consistent performance in the interchangeability of thermocouples is an important feature for achieving high production yields and reducing costs.

An example in glass forming is useful for understanding the combination of key concepts: the need for stringent levels of accuracy in temperature measurement to ascertain product quality and to ensure consistent performance required in the interchangeability of thermocouples. Viscosity of molten glass is the key technical parameter in forming picture tubes used in televisions. Levels of viscosity cannot be measured directly. Measuring the absolute accuracy of the glass softening point to within 1 °C is important for obtaining the desired mechanical properties of the glass. As well, uniform levels of viscosity, obtained through repeatable temperature measurements with interchangeable thermocouples, are important when ensuring consistent quality in manufacturing glass picture tubes.

Generally, the number of calibrations and the quality of calibrations have been increasing industry-wide. The primary reason for this trend is the increased number of organizations seeking higher levels of quality in their products and processes. In particular, the need for traceability to standards, which is one key requirement for achieving certification and audit approval under ISO 9000, has been a driving force for increases in the quantity and quality of thermocouple calibrations. The industrial literature also cites the increased need for tighter measurement tolerances and quality in applications involving health, safety, hygiene, and process control.

Large differences in the market price between thermocouples made from base-metals and noble-metals often influences users' willingness to pay for calibration testing. Most base-metal types of thermocouples and thermocouple assemblies had a 1996 retail price between $6 and $100 per unit. In comparison, prices of noble-metal thermocouples ranged from $250 to $1,000 per unit. Using estimates from commercial calibration service providers, the cost to perform a calibration test for most types of thermocouples ranges between $40 and $100. Therefore, the percentage of total unit price attributable to calibration is much greater for base-metal thermocouple types than for noble-metal types. This is the primary reason that some users of base-metal thermocouples only perform sample calibrations from large lots. For example, one representative of a thermocouple manufacturing company stated that few calibrations are performed on thermocouples sold to the plastic injection molding industry because base-metal thermocouples are used and temperature sensing requirements are not very stringent; these industrial users rely on the sample calibration data produced by the wire supplier, which is sufficient for most plastic injection molding applications. Some industrial users in the four critical industries noted above require calibration of every base-metal thermocouple. Obviously, the percentage of market price attributable to calibration testing will be higher for this latter class of users.

Industrial Structure

The thermocouple industry consists of wire suppliers and thermocouple suppliers. The downstream customers of the wire suppliers are grouped into two general categories, thermocouple suppliers and thermocouple users that fabricate and assemble thermocouples for their own use. As mentioned previously, the wire suppliers typically perform sample calibrations on each production lot. Depending on the accuracy requirements of a given application, these sample calibrations may or may not be sufficient for users of the thermocouple. Therefore, the supplier or user/producer may perform additional calibrations as necessary. According to NIST, the three major suppliers of base-metal type wire are Carpenter Technology, Harrison Alloys, and Hoskins Manufacturing. The four main suppliers of noble-metal wire are Engelhard Industries, Johnson Matthey, PGP Industries, and Sigmund Cohn Corporation.

Thermocouple suppliers purchase wire from the wire suppliers to fabricate and assemble finished thermocouple products. Steps in fabricating such products include encasing a thermocouple in protective sheathing and adding ancillary hardware such as a connector. Myriad configurations of assembled thermocouples are sold, in turn, to users of thermocouples. The on-line product database of the Thomas Register of American Suppliers lists 305 companies selling thermocouple products.

The available information on characteristics of the domestic thermocouple market is less than complete and current. Also, disparities exist among the few sources of market data that are available. The best available information comes from industry trade periodicals and newsletters that report on activities in the thermocouple industry. Based on such sources we have concluded that total domestic shipments of all electronic temperature devices—thermocouples, RTDs, thermistors, and IC sensors—was $402 million in 1991. And, the U.S. consumption of thermocouples in 1991 was $126 million and it was estimated to be $144 million in 1996. A 1991 report by the German firm, Intechno Consulting AG reported world temperature sensing market sales of $2.5 billion in 1991, with projections over the decade growing at a 6.4 percent average annual rate. Distributionally, 33.4 percent of the 1991 market belonged to the United States, 23.7 to Japan, and 42.7 percent to Europe. Regarding thermocouples, Intechno estimated that the 1991 world market was just over $1 billion.

Thermocouples and thermistors are widely used in the health care industry, particularly for monitoring the core body temperatures of patients in many situations, such as anesthetized surgery, outpatient surgery, trauma centers, intensive care, and in-pain clinics. Market Intelligence, Inc. projected in 1991 that the worldwide biomedical sensor market for disposable thermocouples and thermistors would grow from $63.2 million in 1991 at a 9 percent compound annual rate.

An important part of the industrial structure of the industry is the infrastructure support that it receives. The Thermometry Group with CSTL at NIST develops and applies the process of standards traceability for temperature measurement. The Thermocouple Calibration Program is part of the Thermometry Group's overall research activities. This Group is responsible for realizing, maintaining, improving, and disseminating the national standards of temperature. This responsibility for providing reference data is implemented, according to the Group's mission statement, through the following activities:

(1) Determining the accuracy of the national standards of temperature with respect to fundamental thermodynamic relations,
(2) Calibrating practical standards for the U.S. scientific and technical communities in terms of the primary standards,
(3) Developing methods and devices to assist user groups in the assessment and enhancement of the accuracy of their temperature measurements,
(4) Preparing and promulgating evaluations and descriptions of temperature measurement processes,
(5) Coordinating temperature standards and measurement methods nationally and internationally,
(6) Conducting research towards the development of new concepts for standards, and
(7) Developing standard reference materials for use in precision thermometry.

This listing illustrates that NIST is doing more than simply maintaining standards to ensure that industry has a traceable temperature measurement system. NIST also develops and makes available suitable, appropriate, and meaningful measurement methods that permit organizations to correctly use internal instrumentation and reference standards to perform their needed measurements at the required accuracy.

Several national and international organizations sanction standards for practical temperature measurement. These standards often form the basis of purchase specifications used in commercial trade between users and suppliers of thermocouples. The American Society for Testing and Materials (ASTM) and the Instrument Society of America (ISA) are the primary industrial organizations that sanction thermocouple standards used domestically, and different technical specifications are covered in the standards documents of each organization. The ISA Standard MC-96, for example, has been recognized as an American National Standard, while the related ASTM Standard E-230, is presently under consideration as an American National Standard by the American National Standards Institute (ANSI). The International Electrotechnical Commission's (IEC) standard, IEC 584-1, is the standard used internationally.

The thermocouple standards from ASTM, ISA, and IEC subsume calibration reference tables from NIST. The current versions of ASTM E-230 and IEC 584-1 have been updated to include NIST's most recent reference tables and functions, while the current ISA MC-96.11 standard contains an earlier version of NIST's reference tables. Therefore, in practice, the benefits of NIST's reference tables are diffused to thermocouple users and producers through the ASTM, ISA, and IEC standards rather than through NIST-published documents.

The ASTM, ISA, and IEC standards also include other technical specifications, such as color-coding of the thermoelement wires and the extension wires that are needed in the course of commercial trade between users and suppliers of thermocouple products. NIST contributes little technical work or engineering data for developing these more mundane types of specifications since they are not based on leading-edge measurement technology.

NIST also cooperates with standards laboratories in other countries to ensure full compatibility on basic measurement standards used in international trade. While the standards bodies governing various countries agree on both the International Temperature Scale and NIST's reference functions and tables for thermocouple calibration, disagreements often occur on allowable tolerances relative to these reference tables. U.S. tolerances are specified in the ISA and ASTM standards. Developing international consensus on thermometer tolerances is one part of the charters of the IEC and the Organization of Legal Metrology, and NIST participates in both of these international organizations.

Companies that market commercial calibration services comprise another facet of the thermocouple industrial infrastructure. The objectivity of a neutral third party is often valued in negotiations or disputes between suppliers and producers of thermocouples, and the requirement of traceability can avoid potential disagreements or misinterpretations of data. The strength of competitive factors such as pricing, quality, and turn-around time generally determine whether thermocouple users and producers seeking third-party calibration testing use these secondary-level calibration service providers rather than the primary-level services of NIST. Industry representatives concur that NIST provides the highest level of standards traceability for achieving the highest quality calibrations. Yet, many are sensitive to the price of calibration services and perceive the cost of NIST's services as relatively high for their specific needs. However, one of NIST's strategic thrusts is to have its primary standards leverage the private sector provision of secondary standards.

Traceability of Standards

In the overall hierarchy of standards for thermocouple calibration, NIST is viewed as the provider of primary standards from which subordinate reference standards are traced. In the context of measurement science, the system of providing a thoroughly documented unbroken chain of references to a measurement authority is known as traceability.

In the traceability scheme, the users often rely on the proficiency and cost-effectiveness of suppliers or a calibration laboratory in the private sector to obtain calibration. To certify the accuracy of the relationship between temperature and thermoelectric emf for the thermocouple, suppliers must have direct access to appropriate reference standards calibrated in terms of the primary temperature standards maintained at NIST. The producer or commercial laboratory maintains these reference standards internally and compares them with the national standards to achieve traceability.

Organizations that perform internal calibrations of thermocouples employ several general methods to demonstrate and certify traceability to NIST's national temperature standards. Sometimes a temperature measurement is rendered traceable via more than one method. In the first and the most common method, the organization has its thermocouple materials calibrated against the national or primary standard maintained at NIST. These materials then serve as the reference standards or artifacts for internal calibration purposes within the organization. The second established but less common method involves measurement and certification using test methods and apparatus of similar quality to what is employed by NIST. The third and most recent method for thermocouple calibration involves the organization's acquisition of a standard reference material (SRM) from NIST. The SRM is then used as the artifact for internal calibrations.

Users of thermocouples employ one or a combination of strategies in the procurement and calibration of thermocouples depending on their operating practices and accuracy requirements. Users that purchase assembled thermocouples from suppliers generally rely completely on the calibration data provided by the supplier to ensure specified levels of quality. When accuracy beyond the calibration warranties of the suppliers is needed, in-house calibrations are done.

ECONOMIC IMPACT ASSESSMENT

Scope of the Evaluation

NIST has a long history of developing and publishing reference functions and tables for letter-type thermocouples. NIST has updated these reference data with periodic changes in the International Temperature Scale. The most current reference functions and tables for the eight standard letter-type thermocouples were published in NIST Monograph 175 (Burns 1993). These reference data are derived from actual thermoelements that conform to the requirements of the ITS-90 standard.

NIST's Thermometry Group's Thermocouple Calibration Program (TCP) provides primary calibration services for the suppliers and users of thermocouples to achieve levels of measurement accuracy necessary to attain objectives of quality, productivity, and competitiveness. These services constitute the highest order of thermocouple calibration available in the U.S. for customers seeking traceability and conformity to national and international standards. NIST provides these services at a charge equal to the direct cost of the calibration, plus surcharges to offset related fixed costs.

All types of thermocouples, including both letter-designated and non-standard types, can be calibrated by NIST from -196 °C to 2,100 °C. Customers provide samples of either bare wire or complete thermocouples to NIST's laboratory. NIST calibrates these samples on the ITS-90 using one or a combination of different test methods depending on the thermocouple type, the temperature range, and the required accuracy. The calibrated thermocouple is then shipped back to the customer along with a NIST Report of Calibration containing the test procedures and the results of the calibration. The sample and the data from the NIST Report constitute the traceable link to national temperature standards. For example, customers of NIST's primary calibration services can use their calibrated artifact and the accompanying calibration data from the NIST Report as the secondary standard for internal quality control purposes. This secondary reference standard links subsequent calibrations made within the customer's metrology regime to the primary standards maintained by NIST, and thereby to the measurement of other organizations. Such traceability to standards allows the highest level of fidelity for the organization's internal calibrations.

The technical knowledge that forms the foundation for NIST's calibration services is upgraded continuously to improve the traceability process. These improvements are generally in the forms of research on test methods and procedures as well as upgraded equipment, instrumentation, and facilities.

Experts at NIST are available regularly to assist in solving specific problems for industrial organizations. Such problems often pertain to performing thermocouple calibrations or using thermocouples in a temperature measuring system. Direct help is available over the telephone, and NIST estimates that it receives between 20 and 25 telephone calls per week, and by site visits to the Thermometry Group's laboratory.

NIST's specialized expertise in calibration test methods and procedures is particularly sought by industry. Organizations with internal metrology laboratories often seek technical know-how from NIST in establishing and maintaining sound test methods for thermocouple calibrations. These organizations benefit from the research undertaken at NIST to establish primary calibration services, as discussed above. To achieve high levels of traceability internally, some organizations perform secondary-level calibrations by replicating test techniques and apparatus used at NIST.

Periodically, NIST conducts tutorials on thermocouple calibration through conferences and seminars. These tutorials provide education and promote good measurement practices at all levels throughout industry. NIST also provides advice and assistance on problems in thermocouple measurement and calibration as a part of a precision thermometry workshop held twice a year in the NIST Gaithersburg laboratories. Additionally, technical papers regarding NIST research in the measurement field are disseminated at conferences organized by various scientific and engineering groups.

Benefit Measures

Based on background interviews for this case study with NIST experts and several thermocouple users and suppliers, the working hypothesis for the case study was that the infrastructural outputs attributable to NIST's TCP provide users and suppliers with three main types of benefits:

(1) Efficiency in developing the infrastructural technology necessary for calibrating thermocouples is increased. NIST's TCP has obviated the need for duplicative research by individual companies and industry consortia that would have to accept such responsibilities in the absence of the TCP.

(2) Cost and time spent in resolving disputes between users and suppliers involved in thermocouple commerce are reduced. These efficiencies are based on

industrial agreements for the technical basis of standards established through NIST. These agreements are mainly because of industry's recognition of NIST's high quality outputs and impartial competitive posture.

(3) Competitiveness for domestic thermocouple users in the form of better marketability is improved. Competitiveness in this regard is synonymous with calibration accuracy through standards traceable to NIST.

These benefits were simply characterized in Chapter 5 as outcomes related to increased product quality and reduced transaction costs.

Comparison Scenarios

The approach for evaluating the economic benefits associated with the NIST TCP relies on the counterfactual evaluation model. It is assumed that the first-level economic benefits associated with the NIST TCP can be approximated in terms of the additional costs that industry would have incurred in the absence of NIST's services.

The counterfactual experiment is used because this case study lacks a comparable business baseline period prior to the development of NIST's infratechnology outputs. NIST, through its mandated mission, has been the sole provider of these infratechnology outputs to U.S. industry for many years. With respect to the reference tables, no substitute or near-substitute set of outputs exists. Conflicting proprietary tables were in use during the two decades between 1920 and 1940, but obviously that situation no longer exists as industry has relied on NIST for reference tables for letter-designated thermocouples. Therefore, a recent pre-NIST baseline for reference tables is not available for comparison to a post-NIST scenario.

For primary calibration services, a similar situation exists because NIST has been the sole provider of such services since the early 1960s. Commercial calibration services noted above are not a comparable substitute since these commercial organizations themselves rely on the laboratory capabilities of NIST for primary measurement standards.

Absent an actual state-of-practice from an earlier period, a significant part of the economic analysis framework needs to be based on how industry would respond in the counterfactual situation that NIST ceased to provide thermocouple infratechnology outputs.

Benefit Information and Data

Two surveys were conducted for the purposes of collecting information on the economic benefits associated with NIST-supported infratechnologies for thermocouple calibration. One survey focused on thermocouple users and a second on members of the thermocouple industry.

Thermocouple Users

A background survey of 10 thermocouple users was conducted to gain insights regarding calibration practices and perceptions of the value received from NIST's TCP. Many users rely on assurances of thermocouple accuracy from calibration tests performed internally rather than from statements of accuracy from their suppliers. This reliance on internal calibrations is not because of concerns about the process of standards traceability through the NIST TCP. Users have confidence in both NIST measurement and standards capabilities and in the ability of suppliers to calibrate thermocouples that are traceable to national temperature standards. Instead, three general factors regarding the stated accuracy of calibration data from suppliers caused concern.

The first factor relates to the practical aspects of calibrations for thermocouple wire and assembled thermocouples in user applications. The emf versus temperature relationship of two given thermoelements can change by several degrees during the process of fabricating these wires into a thermocouple with sheathing. This change in the calibration of the thermocouple often is not warranted by the supplier, and the variation from thermocouple to thermocouple can be significant. Users control this variation in their instrumentation by establishing offset values that correlate with reference standards calibrated to NIST's primary standards. Many users feel that this random variation in calibration tolerances of thermocouples is accounted for most efficiently through internal calibration activity. As a result, many firms have corporate policies of calibrating the majority, if not all, thermocouples purchased from suppliers. This is done because the use of faulty thermocouple products in user applications could result in incorrect temperature measurements which lead invariably to losses in productivity that greatly exceed the cost of a calibration test.

The second factor relates to users' concerns about the quality of wire procured from wire suppliers. Wire suppliers typically fabricate each production lot in a large spool that is divided subsequently into smaller spools for sale to thermocouple suppliers and users with captive production capabilities. The supplier calibrates wire lengths from the ends of each spool. Often the calibration of wire within the spool deviates beyond an allowable tolerance range from the calibrations performed on the end lengths. Such deviations have made some users unwilling to rely on the supplier's sample calibrations as representative of the entire wire spool, which results in users performing additional calibrations internally. According to one user, substantial oversight of the operations of a wire supplier would be required before both putting greater trust in the supplier's claims on product quality and subsequently lessening its in-house validation testing.

The third factor relates to users' concerns about supplier quality that are not measurement related. Several users claim that their suppliers have made errors in material handling that result in misrepresentation of thermocouple accuracy, incorrect labeling or color-coding of the wires and making a thermocouple with two identical wires. The occurrence of such errors has driven some firms to increase their own validation testing of incoming thermocouple products.

The calibration requirements of thermocouple users generally have remained constant or increased slightly during the 1990s, and compliance with the ISO 9000 quality control scheme has been the driving force for most increases in calibration requirements. Certification to ISO 9000 standards is particularly important in commerce with European and Asian countries. Establishing a process for documenting the accuracy of temperature measurements to national temperature standards is an essential element in meeting ISO 9000 certification. The standards traceability process through the NIST TCP provides thermocouple users with an efficient means to comply with the requirements of ISO 9000 because the burden-of-proof for documented compliance can be obtained from the wire or thermocouple supplier.

Users have realized few net benefits from thermocouples calibrated to the ITS-90 compared to thermocouples calibrated to the previous temperature scale, IPTS-68. The ITS-90 is more accurate than the IPTS-68 and this improved accuracy has been incorporated into the latest reference tables and functions from NIST. However, users generally have not gained improvements in product performance or process efficiencies to offset the costs to incorporate the new calibration standards based on the improved NIST infrastructure technology. In fact, some users have processes that are not sensitive enough to changes in the new scale to warrant the costs of changing their instrumentation to the new standard.

These findings corroborate the views of several thermocouple suppliers during the pretest of the survey instrument. One supplier estimated that 99 percent of all users would be unable to discern the difference in their applications between ITS-90 and IPTS-68 calibrations, and the greater accuracy incorporated in ITS-90 calibrations would probably benefit less than one percent of users having thermocouples calibrated to IPTS-68. Further, many of the thermocouple users undergo the conversion in their internal metrology infrastructure in order to maintain just one set of standards (they use other devices besides thermocouples for measuring temperature, and these other devices do need to be calibrated with ITS-90 standards) even though they are aware that this conversion will not provide a positive economic effect apart from administrative savings.

NIST's role in the standards traceability process reduces transaction costs with suppliers of thermocouple products since procurement disputes between thermocouple users and producers seldom occur. Also, having NIST make the more technically-difficult, highly-accurate temperature measurements in the standards traceability scheme allows thermocouple users to establish and maintain practical calibration standards with equipment and techniques of much lower cost than those used at NIST.

Thermocouple Suppliers

Wire suppliers and thermocouple suppliers were defined for this study as the first-level users of NIST's calibration services, and hence were the relevant survey population for collecting primary benefit data. Based on self-reported market share information the sample of seven wire suppliers represents nearly 100 percent of the

1997 estimated $160 million domestic industry. The sample of twelve thermocouple suppliers represents over 90 percent of the 1997 estimated $120 million domestic market. Since over 300 domestic thermocouple suppliers actively market thermocouple products, the industrial base of thermocouple suppliers appears to be distributed very unevenly.

Opinions of the seven wire suppliers were mixed regarding their company's reaction to the counterfactual scenario of NIST ceasing to provide primary calibration services. Four of the seven thought that their company would rely on foreign laboratories for calibration services similar to those provided by the NIST TCP. Two believed that over time an industry consensus on measurement methods would develop through a private laboratory or industry association; the emerging entity would then assume NIST's current role in providing primary calibration services. One company had no opinion.

Respondents believed that interactions with a foreign laboratory would incur additional, permanent transaction costs under the counterfactual experiment. Based on previous interactions with foreign laboratories, these costs would be associated with both the administrative red tape and inaccessibility of scientists in the foreign laboratories. Although the quality and price of the calibration services from such laboratories are deemed comparable to NIST, the red tape and the delays experienced in receiving services would be significant.

Those respondents anticipating that an industry consensus would develop over time, and the mean response time was estimated to be five years, also anticipated that during this interval a greater number of measurement disputes would arise between their company and their customers and company resources would have to be devoted to the process of reaching industry consensus. Consequently, additional personnel would be needed during this five year interval until the domestic industry reached consensus about acceptable calibration measurements. Examples of the expected types of additional administrative costs included auditing, changes in calibration procedures, and overseas travel. Each wire supplier was asked to approximate, in current 1996 dollars, the additional person-years of effort required to cope with the additional transaction difficulties that would be expected in the absence of the NIST TCP. Each respondent was also asked to value a fully-burdened person-year of labor within their company. The total for all respondents of the additional annual costs that would be needed to address this collection of transaction costs issues, absent NIST's TCP, was $325,000.

In addition to calibration services, the NIST TCP also provides telephone technical support to industry. Each respondent was queried about the frequency with which they took advantage of this service, and on average it was five times per year. Each respondent was also asked about the cost to acquire and utilize this form of NIST information (i.e., pull costs), and in general the response was that the cost was minimal. Absent NIST's services, wire suppliers would purchase similar expertise from consultants, and the total annual cost for all wire suppliers for these substitute benefits was estimated to be $146,500.

Thus, based on the collective opinion of the seven wire suppliers, which effectively represent the entire domestic industry, if NIST's TCP ceased to provide calibration services, this segment of the thermocouple industry would incur $471,500 of additional personnel costs annually to continue to operate at the same level of measurement accuracy.

Similar counterfactual data were collected from the twelve thermocouple suppliers. Regarding an alternative measurement source in the absence of NIST's calibration services, only two respondents thought that their company would rely on a foreign laboratory for calibrations. The other ten respondents believed that an industry consensus would eventually emerge, and similar to the mean reply from the wire suppliers the mean length of time for this to occur was estimated at five years.

The total additional costs during the adjustment interval for the thermocouple suppliers was estimated to be $1,543,400 annually. Also, the total additional cost for the market alternatives to the technical support received from NIST was estimated to be $172,500 annually. Thus, based on interviews with twelve thermocouple suppliers, which effectively represents the domestic industry on a market share basis, if the NIST TCP ceased to provide calibration services then this segment of the industry would incur $1,715,900 in additional annual costs to continue to operated at the same level of measurement accuracy.

Forecast Analysis

Table 7.2 shows NIST's expenditures from 1990 through 1996, along with forecasts through 2001 based on an annual rate of cost increase of six percent, needed to provide the output services described above. These outputs, briefly, include the research on basic physical properties that underlie the measurement science to incorporate change from IPTS-68 to ITS-90. For this effort, NIST led the development of, and shared the cost with the standards laboratories in eight other countries. NIST's costs accounted for about 60 percent of the total expenditures required to generate the updated reference tables. Also, costs for technical support are accounted for in this total.

Fiscal year 1990 was selected as the first year for consideration of NIST costs because it was the year of the most recent update of the international agreements on the scale of temperature, ITS-90, for use in science and industry, and the current state of thermocouple calibration measurement is based on the development of reference tables beginning in that year. NIST began its share of investments in new research in FY90 for upgrading thermocouple reference tables to ensure that U.S. firms could trace their thermocouple product accuracy to the ITS-90. While pre-1990 NIST expenditures have certainly enriched the broadly-defined state of current technical knowledge for thermocouple calibrations, for purposes of our evaluation those expenditures were a sunk cost, and we have addressed the question of whether the post-1990 research—that allowed NIST to maintain its preeminence as the state-of-the-art primary source of standards for thermocouple calibration—was worthwhile. Hence, 1990 was selected as the logical starting point for the comparison of NIST's new post-ITS-90 investment costs to net industry benefits from having NIST's TCP as the source of the primary standards.

Also shown in Table 7.2 are annual estimates of industrial benefits for 1997 through 2001 from the investments made by NIST to establish its current state-of-the-art reference tables and to maintain its expertise and services. These data are based on the 1996 estimate of industrial benefits totaling $2,187,400 from above: $471,500 from the wire suppliers plus $1,715,900 from the thermocouple suppliers. The estimates reported in the table are an extrapolation for five years using what industry reported as a reasonable annual rate of fully-burdened labor cost increase over that period, five percent. To be conservative, benefits prior to 1997 are omitted to ensure that the NIST investments to develop the new ITS-90 based reference tables and services were fully in place. The five year forecast period was selected for two reasons. One, five years represents the average amount of time that respondents projected for the thermocouple industry to reach a consensus on an alternative to NIST's calibration services in the counterfactual experiment, that in this case was: if NIST's TCP were abandoned now, to what alternative would your company turn and how long would it take to reach a consensus that replaced NIST's TCP infrastructure. Two, although some respondents believed that the additional transaction costs would exist forever if companies relied on foreign laboratories and although market consulting alternatives for technical assistance would likewise exist forever, truncating such benefits at five years makes the performance evaluation metrics presented below conservative and certainly lower-bound estimates.

Table 7.2. NIST TCP Costs and Industrial Benefits

Fiscal Year	NIST Costs	Industrial Benefits
1990	$220,400	
1991	325,900	
1992	483,200	
1993	266,600	
1994	206,100	
1995	211,800	
1996	174,700	
1997	185,200	$2,296,800
1998	196,300	2,411,600
1999	208,100	2,532,200
2000	220,600	2,658,800
2001	233,800	2,791,800

Performance Evaluation Metrics

Table 7.3 summarizes the three NIST performance evaluation metrics, discussed in Chapter 4, using a discount rate equal to 7 percent plus the average annual rate of inflation from 1990 through 1996; 2.96 percent. Certainly, on the basis of these metrics the TCP investments have been worthwhile.

Table 7.3. NIST TCP Performance Evaluation Metrics

Performance Evaluation Metric	Estimate (rounded)
Internal rate of return	32%
Implied rate of return	21%
Ratio of benefits-to-costs	3

CONCLUSIONS

Recall again Chapter 3's explanation of the counterfactual method. The performance evaluation metrics for the counterfactual method as reported in Table 7.3 show that NIST carried out the post-ITS-90 development more efficiently than would have been the case if the private sector had made the investments instead. As explained in Chapter 3, that is not the same thing as saying that to date the investments have generated a high rate of return. Survey information provided evidence that the vast majority of thermocouple users—including users with high accuracy requirements—have attained few benefits from using thermocouples calibrated to the ITS-90 compared to thermocouples calibrated to the IPTS-68. Theoretically, the greater accuracy embedded in the improved temperature scale would allow thermocouple users with high accuracy requirements to obtain enhanced product performance and process efficiencies because the ITS-90 is more accurate thermodynamically than the IPTS-68. The upgrade of thermocouple reference tables and functions to facilitate the conversion from IPTS-68 to ITS-90 is one of the outputs being evaluated in this case study, hence follow-up information regarding this issue is warranted.

Two sets of investments have been made in the conversion of standards for thermocouple calibration that are consistent with the improvements in the technical state-of-the-art of the international temperature scale from IPTS-68 to ITS-90. The first set of investments has been made collectively by agreements among NIST and the standards laboratories of eight other countries, and these investments led to the upgrade of the reference tables and functions for thermocouples calibrated to the ITS-90. The second set of investments has been made by all organizations that converted internal measurement infrastructures to the ITS-90. Using the anecdotal results from the survey of thermocouple users, the intrinsic return from both sets of investments has been poor.

The investment decision by NIST to upgrade the reference tables was driven by international agreements on the change in the temperature scale. While the economic returns to industry on this investment to date have not been significant, the original decision must be assessed relative to the economic consequences of not having made the investment. As was done in this case study, the evaluation of economic impacts is posed in terms of the likely scenario and qualitative consequences to industry if NIST had not invested and participated in upgrading the thermocouple reference tables to ITS-90.

According to experts at NIST, the primary motivation for NIST's original investment decision made cooperatively with the standards organizations of the other eight countries was to ensure that all thermocouple users and producers would maintain the same temperature scale for measurements. The decision contributes to consistency in the national standards for temperature among the United States and other industrial countries that seek leading-edge measurement technology to augment advanced technology products.

Under a counterfactual scenario of NIST having not participated in the joint investments, U.S. companies would likely have risked being able to sell their products in certain international markets. This risk is likely to have been greater for the population of thermocouple users in comparison to the smaller population of thermocouple suppliers and wire suppliers since the product sales outside of the United States for the latter set of producers are not significant.

The ITS-90 affects all devices for measuring temperature. Many organizations that use thermocouples also use other types of temperature measuring devices for internal applications. Given the over-arching acceptance of the ITS-90, the temperature measurement community has agreed that investments in upgraded calibration knowledge were necessary for all temperature measurement devices. If such investments were not made for every device, then users would be faced with making in-house temperature measurements with more than one temperature scale. Thus, seen in the broad context of international trade and the international standards community, NIST's investments to keep its thermocouple calibration capabilities state-of-the-art and consistent with those of the international community have benefits that would not typically have materialized as improved product or process performance from greater accuracy in temperature measurement from a narrow perspective about an individual thermocouple product or process. Furthermore, and most importantly, in the absence of the post-ITS-90 investments, NIST would not have been able to maintain its role as the authority to which thermocouple calibration standards are traced.

8 SOFTWARE ERROR COMPENSATION RESEARCH*

INTRODUCTION

The technology of manufacturing accuracy has deep roots in American economic history. In the mid-19th century, British observers commented on a uniquely American approach to manufacturing, an approach referred to as the "American System of Manufacturing" (Rosenberg, 1972). The essence of the "American System" was the standardization and interchangeability of manufactured items. This approach to manufacturing was fundamentally different from the British approach, which stressed labor-intensive customization by highly-skilled craftsmen.

Interchangeability presumed manufacturing precision, and interchangeability therefore greatly reduced the very costly state of fitting activities by moving toward a simpler assembly process that required little more than a turnscrew. Interchangeable components, the elimination of dependence upon handicraft skills, and the abolition of extensive fitting operations were all aspects of a manufacturing system whose fundamental characteristic was the design and utilization of highly specialized machinery.

The evolution of specialized machines brought about by the emphasis on interchangeability was abetted by the evolution of the technology of measurement. And, as cheaper and more effective measurement devices became available, not only did the degree of interchangeability achieved in manufacturing increase, but also the production of the specialized machinery itself became a specialized activity undertaken by a well-defined group of firms in the manufacturing sector. The development and use of measurement technology is, as economic historians have noted, an important part of industrial history. The coordinate measurement machine (CMM) is in many respects the culmination of the development of dimensional measurement technology.

The concept of interchangeable parts necessitated the creation of the concept of part tolerance. And, the ability to produce large numbers of parts of sufficiently

---

* This chapter was co-authored with David P. Leech. See Leech and Link (1996).

small variation is based on the ability to measure such variation accurately. The development of software error compensation (SEC) through the research in dimensional metrology in the Precision Engineering Division within the National Institute of Standards and Technology's (NIST's) Manufacturing Engineering Laboratory (MEL) was, in large part, a response to the metrological demands of discrete part manufacturers for ever-increasing manufacturing accuracy and precision.

A CMM, and its associated SEC technology, is part of a so-called second industrial revolution that first became evident in the 1960s. This revolution was based on the application of science to industrial processes and the development of unified systems of automated industrial control. Clearly, NIST's development of SEC technology is an important part of this historical process. In fact, informed observers suggest that the application benefits of SEC technology go well beyond CMMs to a variety of cutting and forming machine tools, and these broader benefits have only begun to be realized.

This case study assesses the first-order economic impacts associated with the development and initial diffusion of SEC technology to producers of CMMs.

MARKET FOR COORDINATE MEASURING MACHINES

Evolution of Dimensional Measurement Technology

CMMs are the culmination of the technological evolution of dimensional measurement. Thus, they are integrally related to the evolution of manufacturing technology.

Measurement technology is fundamental to modern industrial life; it is an ever-present reality for discrete part manufacturers. Conformance of manufactured parts to increasingly precise specifications is fundamental to U.S. manufacturers remaining competitive in the world market.

Familiarity with basic industrial measurement devices is useful background to understanding the significance of CMMs and, in particular, the introduction and application of SEC technology.

A wide variety of gaging and measuring devices are employed in a contemporary manufacturing environment, including probes, rules, squares, calipers, micrometers, all manner of gages, gage blocks, automatic sorting systems, lasers, optical and mechanical comparators, flatness testers, interferometers, and coordinate measurement machines. The functions performed by a CMM have historically been performed with some combination of the types of individual mechanical measuring devices listed, but not as flexibly, quickly, or accurately.

The choice of a measurement tool depends on the sensitivity and resolution required in the measurement. Perhaps the most basic of all measuring devices is the ruler; a standard of length. The steel rule, sometimes referred to as a scale, remains even today as the primary factory measuring tool. A common commercial variation of the steel rule is the combination square. In addition to its use for direct linear measurement, the combination square is used to assess angles and depths. Calipers and micrometers are also traditional measurement devices for assessing dimensional accuracy. They are generally used in combination with, or as an accessory to, the steel rule especially in the measurement of diameter and thickness. The first practical mechanic's micrometer was, according to Bosch (1995), marketed in the United States by Brown & Sharpe in 1867.

Precision gage blocks are another common measurement technology. Commercial gage blocks are steel blocks, hardened with carefully machined parallel and flat surfaces. They are used to build various gaging lengths. Great care is taken in the manufacturing of these devices to ensure flat, parallel measuring surfaces. The gage blocks are graded for various levels of accuracy, ranging from the master blocks (highest accuracy) to the working blocks (lowest accuracy).

The surface plate is another measurement building block. It can be made of cast iron, granite, or glass. Set level on a bench stand with its one flat, polished surface facing upward, a surface plate provides the X-axis in a measurement set-up.

Comparators combine any number of the above measurement instruments in a test set-up that allows the comparison of unknown with known dimensions. For complex parts requiring measurement in three dimensions, the comparator consists of instruments which, integrated as a single measuring set-up, constitute X, Y, and Z measurement axes. The basic comparator consists of a surface plate or flat surface for the X-axis, a test set or fixture for the Y-axis, and an indicator for the Z-axis.

Coordinate Measuring Machines

In one respect, CMMs are little more than a refinement of the above gaging and measurement equipment. CMMs combine many of the features of traditional measuring devices into one integrated, multi-functional measuring machine. In another respect, they are a major breakthrough in mechanizing the inspection process and in lowering inspection costs. They provide three-dimensional measurements of the actual shape of a work piece; its comparison with the desired shape; and the evaluation of metrological information such as size, form, location, and orientation.

The automation of machine tools in the 1950s and 1960s created the need for a faster and more flexible means of measuring manufactured parts. Parts made in a matter of minutes on the then new numerically-controlled machines took hours to inspect. This inspection requirement resulted in a new industry for three-dimensional measuring machines. More recently, the emphasis on statistical process control for quality improvement has accelerated the demand for faster and more accurate measurements.

The economic importance of CMMs comes from their ability to compute from the measured points in a three-dimensional space any one of a whole family of dimensional quantities such as position of features relative to part coordinates, distance between features, forms of features, and angular relationships between features.

Economic Role of CMMs

From a strategic business perspective, the ultimate value of a CMM is derived from its flexibility and ability to execute production control. Quality is identified as a key strategic imperative for many manufacturers, and process control is at the heart of quality assurance. CMMs provide such control cost effectively. Table 8.1 summarizes the advantages of coordinate metrology through CMMs compared to traditional metrology.

Table 8.1. Traditional and Coordinate Metrology Procedures

Traditional Metrology	Coordinate Metrology
Manual, time-consuming alignment of the test piece	Alignment of the test piece is not necessary
Single-purpose and multi-point measuring instruments make it difficult to adapt to changing measurement tasks	Simple adaptation to the measuring tasks by software
Comparison of measurements with standard measurement fixtures is required	Comparison of measurements with mathematical or numerical models
Different machines required to perform determination of size, form, location, and orientation	Determination of size, form, location, and orientation in one set-up using one reference scale

CMMs are most frequently used for quality control and shop floor production inspections. A 1993 survey of use that was published in *Production Magazine* is summarized in Table 8.2. Based on the information in Table 8.2, CMMs are used least frequently in metrology laboratories.

Table 8.2. Functional Applications of CMMs

Function	Frequency
Quality control	30%
Shop floor production inspection	24
Tooling	17
Receiving inspection	17
Metrology laboratory activity	10

Although no published governmental data exist, a 1989 survey that was published in the *American Machinist* reported that in that year there were nearly 16,000 CMMs being used in the manufacturing sector of the economy, with nearly one-half being used in the production of industrial machinery and equipment, and nearly one-third being used in the production of transportation equipment. And, CMMs are used in plants of a variety of sizes. Nearly 50 percent of all CMMs reported as in use in 1989 were in plants with less than 100 employees. Plants with more than 500 employees accounted for about 25 percent of the usage.

Evolution of the CMM Industry

According to Bosch (1995), the development of CMMs is inextricably linked to the development of automated machine tools. In fact, the first CMM was developed by the Italian company Ferranti, Ltd. as complementary equipment to its numerically-controlled machine tools. In 1956, Harry Ogden, the designer of Ferranti's CMM conceived of a measuring machine that would fundamentally change the economics of conventional inspection methods. Ferranti had not previously been involved in the production of measuring equipment, but entered the market in response to market demand for faster and more flexible measuring needs to complement the use of automated machine tools. Parts made in minutes on automated machine tools initially required hours of inspection. The demand for the Ferranti machine, and its successors, created a large market throughout the industrial world and led to the development of similar machines with larger capacities and improved accuracy and resolution.

Inspired by the Ferranti CMM that was displayed at the 1959 International Machine Tool Show in Paris, France, the Sheffield Division of Bendix Corporation (U.S.) developed and then displayed its CMM in 1960. Soon thereafter, Bendix's customer, Western Electric, compared traditional measurement times to the measurement times of the Bendix CMM and found a 20-fold increase in measurement speed. Reported findings such as that drastically increased the world demand for CMMs, and hence competitors entered the market at an average of two per year for the next 25 years.

In 1962, the Italian company, Digital Electronics Automation (DEA) became the first company established for the exclusive purpose of manufacturing CMMs. DEA delivered its first machine in 1965. In the early 1970s, Brown & Sharpe (U.S.) and Zeiss (German) entered into the CMM market. The Japanese firm, Mititoyo, commercialized its CMM in 1978. Also in that year, Zeiss acquired the newly formed Numerex (U.S.), and Giddings & Lewis (U.S.) acquired Sheffield. In 1992, Ferranti ceased production of CMMs. In 1994, Brown & Sharpe acquired DEA. As of 1995, there were between 25 and 30 CMM manufacturers worldwide, but the $500 million world market was dominated by Brown & Sharpe with a 45 percent market share, followed by Giddings & Lewis and Zeiss each with nearly an 18 percent market share. Most of the other firms service niche markets. The U.S. market is approximately one-half of the world market in terms of sales.

SOFTWARE ERROR COMPENSATION TECHNOLOGY

The Competitive Environment

The evolution of the CMM industry is not significantly different from that of many technologically-sophisticated industries. As described in the previous section, its history is one of entry and consolidation. In large part, the development of this industry has been driven by the pace of complementary technological developments in other industries, most notable the computer and machine tool industries. In addition to its organic connection to these two industries, the CMM industry has been driven by the global emphasis on higher quality in all areas of manufacturing.

For some manufacturers, precision is extremely important and demands for increasing precision are a dominant competitive force. Continued competitiveness in the global market makes the ability to manufacture to increasingly tight dimensional tolerances imperative. As evidenced by Japan's success over the past decades in automobiles, machine tools, video recorders, microelectronic devices, and other super-precision products, improvements in dimensional tolerances and product quality are a major factor in achieving dominance of markets.

Software Error Compensation

SEC technology is a computer-based mathematical technique for increasing the accuracy of CMMs. SEC technology embedded in a CMM's controller's software embodies four essential elements:

(1) Knowledge of error sources in the CMM's automated measuring process,
(2) A mathematical model of the CMM,
(3) A metrology of measurement to provide data to the model, and
(4) A metrology for implementing the model in the CMM analysis computer.

In other words, the CMM itself may be imprecise because of imperfections in its construction or in how it varies in accuracy in different thermal conditions. SEC technology corrects for these factors to increase the accuracy of the CMM. SEC technology addresses what metrologists call quasistatic errors of relative position between the CMM probe—the part of the CMM that contacts the object being measured to establish its true position and dimensions—and the work piece (Hocken 1993).

Technical Significance of SEC

The SEC concept revolutionized the traditional approach to improving the accuracy of CMMs and other precision machines. Metrology experts distinguish two broad error-reduction strategies, error avoidance and error compensation. Error avoidance seeks to eliminate the sources of error through greater precision in the manufacture of machine parts. Error compensation seeks to cancel the effect without eliminating its source.

Historically, error compensation was achieved by adding mechanical devices to a machine. For example, throughout the 19th century machine tool users rotated a lead screw to move a nut along a set of tracks. By rotating the lead screw, the nut moved linearly and thereby compensated for errors in the manufacture of the machine tool. However, there could be errors in the manufacture of the screw, such as imprecision in the number of threads per inch. Thus, additional compensation would be needed, and so on. With SEC, all error related information is stored in software and that software compensates for all errors associated with a CMM.

From an economic perspective, as precision tolerances have become less and less forgiving, investments in error avoidance have increased. This fact, and the cost associated with error avoidance, is the basis for the appeal and widespread acceptance of error compensation. SEC allows CMM to add error-compensation to error-avoidance strategies to achieve efficient error-reduction in the manufacture of machine parts.

NIST'S ROLE IN THE DEVELOPMENT AND DIFFUSION OF SEC

Between 1975 and 1985, NIST was engaged in a number of projects related to the development and demonstration of SEC technology. Based on an interview with Robert Hocken, the first project leader of NIST's SEC research effort:

> The fundamental mission of NIST's Manufacturing Engineering Laboratory was to push the state-of-the-art in measurement. The CMMs available to NIST at the time the project began were the very best but they were not good enough. Gage blocks, the conventional measurement technology at the time, were far more accurate than CMMs.

Because the traditional measurement technology was slow and inflexible, and because CMMs were not well respected in the industrial communities, NIST concluded that CMM accuracy needed to be improved and SEC was the technology needed to do it.

One persistent theme in the interviews associated with this case study was that the CMM industry was very conservative while in its infancy, and the CMM industry was unwilling to make the necessary investments to explore and demonstrate the feasibility of the SEC approach to improving CMM accuracy. Accordingly, during the 1975 to 1985 period, NIST research contributed the following to the development of SEC technology:

(1) Demonstrated to industry the feasibility of three-dimensional software error correction for CMMs,
(2) Implemented SEC on a relatively low cost CMM design,

(3) Provided extensive explanation and consultation to producers and users of CMMs concerning the need for SEC and its practicality,
(4) Demonstrated and explained to CMM producers the mathematics of how to construct the equations and how to solve the problem technically, and
(5) Demonstrated a systematic approach to gathering and organizing the data for practical purposes and implemented a straightforward approach to software implementation.

A recent historical review of the scientific literature concerning software error compensation concluded that the most common current methods of SEC had their origin at NIST (Hocken 1993). Industry representatives active in the market at the time of NIST's SEC efforts argue that NIST researchers demonstrated what could be done before it was economically feasible to do so commercially. Before SEC could take hold, the price of computer power had to drop to justify the manufacture of CMMs using new designs. Interviews with several of the original NIST researchers as well as numerous industry representatives uniformly describe a very conservative industry mind set that also had to be overcome in order for the acceptance and implementation of this new technology to proceed.

Beginning in the early 1970s, NIST's MEL, under the direction of John Simpson, undertook a project to computerize a relatively impressive CMM, a Moore-M5Z. Hocken joined the project in 1975 and introduced an innovative conceptual approach to software error compensation. This initial work was published in 1977. Over the course of a decade, a number of researchers participated in the project and made individual contributions to the implementation of the original Hocken concept. In addition, industry advisory board representatives, including both Brown & Sharpe and Sheffield, encouraged the development of SEC technology, seeing it as a means of competitive advantage with respect to foreign competitors, Zeiss in particular.

Between 1982 and 1984, the NIST research team succeeded in implementing and documenting three-dimensional error compensation on a commercial type of machine using the Brown & Sharpe coordinate measuring machine Validator series. These results were made public by NIST researchers in 1985. From NIST's perspective, the importance of the Validator project was that it introduced SEC technology into a widely used and relatively inexpensive CMM design.

Between the original Hocken-inspired efforts and the Validator projects, NIST researchers implemented SEC technology in a number of machine tool applications, including a Brown & Sharpe machine center and a Hardinge turning center.

Commercial introduction of compensated CMMs began in the mid-1980s. U.S. industry representatives place the first commercial introductions around 1984 or 1985, an estimated five to ten years before U.S. firms would have introduced this technology without NIST's efforts. Brown & Sharpe claims to have introduced an early compensated CMM, the Validator-300, in 1984 and another model, the Excell, in 1986. According to industry experts, Zeiss and the Sheffield Division of Bendix were the first to introduce full volumetric compensation on their CMM lines in 1985. For example, Sheffield's 1989 and 1990 patents, "Methods for Calibrating a

Coordinate Measuring Machine and the Like and System Thereof," Patent #4819195, and "Method for Determining Position Within the Measuring Volume of a Coordinate Measuring Machine and System Thereof," Patent #4945501, cite papers by NIST researchers as prior art. And the Brown & Sharpe 1990 patent, "Method for Calibration of Coordinate Measuring Machine," Patent #4939678, cites the first Sheffield patent.

ECONOMIC IMPACT ASSESSMENT

SEC Development Costs

NIST researchers undertook their SEC-related research between 1975 and 1985. Over this decade, a total of seven person-years were committed to the research project. In addition to this investment of time, there was a significant amount of equipment purchased. When NIST's staff was asked for this case study to reproduce the cost budget associated with this research program, no documentation was available. However, retrospectively, NIST staff concurred that the present value, in 1994 dollars, of these seven person-years was $700,000, and the present value of the cost of the equipment was $50,000. NIST's staff also concurred that less labor was used in the early years of the project compared to the latter years. Therefore, for the purpose of constructing a time series of cost data, it was assumed for this case study that 0.5 person-years were devoted to the research project in each year from 1975 through 1980, and then 1.0 person-year in each year from 1981 through 1984. Similarly, it was assumed that all equipment purchases occurred in 1984. To construct each cost data element in Table 8.3, the 1994 dollar estimates were deflated using the Consumer Price Index (1982-1984=100). While the cost data in Table 8.3 represent the best institutional information available, they are retrospectively constructed.

First-Order Economic Benefits

The first-order economic benefits quantified in this study relate to the feasibility research cost savings and related efficiency gains in research and production to CMM producers resulting from the availability of the NIST quality control algorithm. It was concluded from interviews with representatives from domestic CMM producers that, in the absence of NIST's research in SEC technology, they would have eventually undertaken the research costs to demonstrate SEC feasibility so as to remain competitive in the world market. These costs were "saved" in the sense that NIST provided the technology to the domestic industry. In the absence of NIST—the counterfactual evaluation method—industry experts estimated that this research would have lagged NIST's research by between five (median response) and six (mean response) years. In other words, without NIST's investments, industry participants would not have begun to develop the relevant SEC technical information on their own until about 1981, whereas NIST's research began in 1975. Industry experts predicted that this research would have likely been undertaken independently by Brown & Sharpe and Sheffield because of their market position and their knowledge that similar efforts were being undertaken by foreign competitors. Other domestic CMM companies would have benefited as the technical knowledge diffused, but these companies were not in a financial position to underwrite such research.

Table 8.3. NIST SEC Research Costs

Year	Person-Years	Labor Costs	Equipment Costs
1975	0.5	$18,200	$ 0
1976	0.5	19,200	0
1977	0.5	20,500	0
1978	0.5	22,000	0
1979	0.5	24,500	0
1980	0.5	27,800	0
1981	1.0	61,300	0
1982	1.0	65,100	0
1983	1.0	67,200	0
1984	1.0	70,100	35,100

In an effort to create an absent-NIST scenario in order to quantify the feasibility research cost savings to the CMM industry, it was assumed that private sector research would have begun in 1981 and would have been completed in 1989, a five year lag in the state of knowledge. Those interviewed at Brown & Sharpe and Sheffield, and at other companies, estimated that they would have expended collectively a total for four person-years of effort between 1981 and 1989. In mid-1995, they valued a fully-burdened person-year at $110,000. Of course, such estimates are forecast with hindsight and might well underestimate the risk of the endeavor and hence the true cost to the industry. Nevertheless, these estimates are the best available.

The data in Table 8.4 represent cost-savings to the CMM industry. In addition, those CMM producers interviewed reported that they also realized efficiency gains because the use of SEC in their CMMs improved their net profits from the sale of CMMs. For the domestic CMM industry, the estimated efficiency gains ranged between 10 percent per year to 30 percent per year beginning in 1985, the year after NIST completed its feasibility research. These gains in production efficiency for the entire CMM industry were estimated by the industry experts at $27 million per year for 1994. We have then quantified an additional value of products that would not have been realized in the absence of NIST's investments in SEC technology. The SEC case, then, is one of those where, as discussed in Chapter 3, the market failures were sufficiently severe to prevent the feasible private-sector replacement investments from completely replicating the results of NIST's research. In this SEC case, the best counterfactual private response was expected to lag NIST's results by five years.

As shown in Table 8.5, the net productivity gains realized by the CMM industry are only for the years 1985 through 1988. NIST's SEC research was completed in 1984, and comparable research undertaken by the CMM industry would have been completed in 1989. The figures for 1985-1988 are derived from the 1994 $27 million per year estimate by deflation using the Consumer Price Index as in Table 8.3.

Table 8.6 shows the NIST research costs associated with the development and diffusion of SEC technology and the CMM industry benefits associated with using that technology. These CMM industry benefits are the sum (using four significant digits) of the industry feasibility research cost savings from Table 8.4 and its net productivity gains from Table 8.5. Net benefits, by year, are the difference between the NIST costs and industry benefits series.

Table 8.4. Industry SEC Research Cost Savings

Year	Work Years	Labor Costs
1981	0.5	$33,700
1982	0.5	35,800
1983	0.5	37,000
1984	0.5	38,600
1985	0.5	39,900
1986	0.5	40,700
1987	0.5	42,200
1988	0.5	43,900

Table 8.5. Net CMM Industry Productivity Gains Resulting from NIST Research

Year	Value of Nominal Productivity Gains
1985	$19,600,000
1986	20,000,000
1987	20,700,000
1988	21,500,000

Performance Evaluation Metrics

Table 8.7 summarizes the value of the three NIST performance evaluation metrics, discussed in Chapter 4, using a discount rate equal to 7 percent plus the average annual rate of inflation from 1975 through 1988; 8.0 percent. Certainly, on the basis of these metrics the SEC research program was worthwhile.

CONCLUSIONS

Although only first-order economic benefits were estimated in this study, it was the consensus opinion of all industry experts that the second-order benefits realized by users of SEC-compensated CMMs are significantly greater in value. Thus, the quantitative findings presented above are a lower-bound of the true benefits to industry resulting from NIST's research in SEC technology.

The second-order benefits of software compensated CMMs will accrue to CMM users. Based on the information discussed above, it is reasonable to expect the benefits of NIST's SEC impacts to be felt by large and small manufacturers alike and to be concentrated in the industrial machinery and equipment and the transportation industries. CMM producers are of the opinion that the benefits to users will take the form of inspection cost savings, reduced scrap rates and related inventory cost savings, and lower CMM maintenance costs.

Table 8.6. NIST SEC Research Costs and CMM Industrial Benefits

Year	NIST Labor and Equipment Costs	Industrial Benefits
1975	$ 18,200	
1976	19,200	
1977	20,500	
1978	22,000	
1979	24,500	
1980	27,800	
1981	61,300	$ 33,700
1982	65,100	35,800
1983	67,200	37,000
1984	105,200	38,600
1985		19,640,000
1986		20,040,000
1987		20,740,000
1988		21,540,000

Table 8.7. NIST SEC Performance Evaluation Metrics

Performance Evaluation Metric	Estimate (rounded)
Internal rate of return	99%
Implied rate of return	62%
Ratio of benefits-to-costs	85

Finally, the first- and second-order benefits of SEC technology are but examples of the total benefits that are likely to have resulted from NIST's focus on dimensional metrology. For example, it has been suggested that the implementation of SEC technology in cutting and forming machine tools has begun and that this implementation represents as significant a change for that segment of the machine tool industry as it has for the CMM industry.

9 CERAMIC PHASE DIAGRAM PROGRAM*

INTRODUCTION

More than 100 years ago, scientists discovered the usefulness of phase diagrams for describing the interactions of inorganic materials in a given system. Phase equilibria diagrams are graphical representations of the thermodynamic relations pertaining to the compositions of materials. Ceramists have long been leaders in the development and use of phase equilibria diagrams as primary tools for describing, developing, specifying, and applying new ceramic materials.

Phase diagrams provide reference data that represent the phase relations under a certain limited set of conditions. A ceramist conducting new materials research will invariably conduct experiments under different conditions than those that underlie the phase diagram. The reference data in the phase diagram provide the user with a logical place to begin experimentation for new research and to bypass certain paths that would lead to a dead end.

For over 60 years, the National Institute of Standards and Technology (NIST) and the American Ceramic Society (ACerS) have collaborated in the collection, evaluation, organization, and replication of phase diagrams for ceramists. This collaboration began in the late 1920s between Herbert Insley of the National Bureau of Standards and F.P. Hall of Pass and Seymour, Inc., a New York-based company. Since that time, over 10,000 diagrams have been published by ACerS through its close working relationship with NIST. The collaboration between these two organizations was informal until December, 1982, and successive formal agreements have extended the program to the present.

This program, within the Materials Science and Engineering Laboratory (MSEL), is known as the Phase Equilibria Program. Its purpose is to support growth and progress in ceramics industries by providing qualified, critically-evaluated data on thousands of chemical systems relevant to ceramic materials research and engineering. This information serves as an objective reference for

---

* This chapter was co-authored with Michael L. Marx. See Marx, Link, and Scott (1998).

important statistical parameters such as melting points and chemical reactivity. In short, the database is a valuable source of infrastructure technology for ceramists in research- and application-oriented organizations.

The intention of the Program is to overcome problems that researchers have in using ceramic phase equilibria diagrams that appear in the various technical journals. For example, the original source of a diagram is often obscure or not available readily to all ceramists. Diagrams are also published with inconsistent styles and units, and some diagrams are published with obvious, at least to expert ceramists, errors in thermodynamic data. Those errors could cause design failures. Maintaining currency of the diagrams is another concern of ceramists. Hence, the objective and scope of the NIST/ACerS program is to compile an accessible, accurate, systematic, and current set of phase diagrams that have already appeared in the archival literature.

PHASE EQUILIBRIA PROGRAM

An understanding of phase equilibria relations is basic in the development and utilization of ceramic materials. Phase equilibria address the flexibility and constraints dictated by forces of nature on the evolution of phase assemblages in ceramics. Phase boundaries also assist in the evaluation of the service stability of a ceramic material, both in the long- and short-time frames. Thus, knowledge of the stability of a ceramic component in high-temperature or high-pressure environments can often be obtained from an appropriate phase diagram.

Phase diagrams yield important information on key processing parameters of ceramics. The chemical and physical properties of ceramic products are related to the number, composition, and distribution of the phases present. Temperature, pressure, and material concentration are the principal variables that determine the kinds and amounts of the phases present under equilibrium conditions. To ceramists, who must understand the effects of these variables on both the processing and the properties of finished ceramic products, the necessary fundamental information of phase equilibrium relations is often provided from phase diagrams.

The Phase Equilibria Program benefits the industrial community of ceramists in a number of ways. The use of accurate, evaluated phase diagrams minimizes design failure, over design, and inefficient processing. Another impact is the reduction in duplicative research performed by individual ceramists. The savings in time and resources to search and evaluate the phase diagrams individually can be directed more productively to applied research on the material of interest. Also, the ready access of qualified diagrams can spur the insertion of ceramic materials into new applications. For example, the availability of high-quality diagrams is credited with the rapid development of ceramic materials used in the cement and metal processing industries.

The primary output of the NIST/ACerS Phase Equilibria Program has been the compilation of evaluated reference data, as was noted in Chapter 5. These data have been published as *Phase Diagrams for Ceramists (PDFC)*, in printed form and, in recent years, in electronic form. The current set of *PDFC* consists of 14 volumes and 11 smaller compilations, and each *PDFC* document encompasses a particular niche of ceramics. ACerS estimates that more than 45,000 copies of the 14-volume set have been sold since first becoming available in 1933.

The Phase Equilibria Program is managed under the Phase Equilibria Program Committee of ACerS. Committee membership includes members of the Society, the ACerS Executive Director and the Chief of the Ceramics Division of MSEL. Other Society and NIST employees serve as important resources to the Committee. Selection of diagrams from the available technical literature is one of the tasks of this Committee. The diagrams selected for evaluation and compilation are meant to meet the pressing needs of researchers and industry.

Under the current joint arrangement, NIST administers the technical aspects of the Program and ACerS oversees the publication of data. The actual evaluation is performed by reviewers from academia, industry, and government laboratories outside of NIST, as well as by consultants. ACerS is responsible for preparing, disseminating and operating database outputs in electronic and printed forms.

The Program is funded through a variety of sources. ACerS contributions come from a mix of endowment income and net proceeds from sales of *PDFC* volumes. NIST provides funding from the MSEL Standard Reference Data Program and the Ceramics Division. Annual expenditure data from 1985 through 1996 are shown in Table 9.1. Research efforts over this time period incorporate nine *PDFC* volumes, six of which relate to advanced ceramics. Note that solely the public funding provided by NIST for the Phase Equilibria Program is included in Table 9.1. For this particular case, the output is in reality the result of a public/private partnership, and the public research expenditures shown in Table 9.1 are combined with the private sector expenditures to produce the output—the *PDFC* volumes—of the NIST/ACerS partnership. Our counterfactual analysis assumes that in the absence of NIST's participation, the ACerS spending to promote use of phase diagrams would continue at about the same level. That is a conservative assumption, because the costs of coordinating and assimilating the existing literature in the absence of NIST's research investments would surely exceed the costs of publishing the *PDFC* volumes. Thus, the additional social costs from having the NIST Phase Equilibria Program are just the NIST expenditures.

ROLE OF PHASE DIAGRAMS IN INDUSTRIAL APPLICATIONS

The evaluation and availability of phase diagrams are extremely important for the economic well-being of the ceramic industry. In the past, industry representatives have estimated that the lack of readily available compilations of evaluated phase diagrams costs industry many millions of dollars per year because of:

(1) Product failures resulting from materials based on unreliable thermodynamic data,
(2) Unnecessary over design and waste,
(3) Inefficient materials processing, and

(4) Needless duplication of research and development costs which occurs when the data sought have already been generated but published in an obscure journal.

Table 9.1. NIST Phase Equilibria Program Research Expenditures

Year	Research Expenditures
1985	$420,000
1986	420,000
1987	382,000
1988	294,000
1989	255,000
1990	265,000
1991	87,000
1992	94,000
1993	103,000
1994	105,000
1995	97,000
1996	136,000

INDUSTRY AND MARKET FOR ADVANCED CERAMICS

Ceramic materials are divided into two general categories, traditional and advanced. Traditional ceramics include clay-based materials such as brick, tile, sanitary ware, dinnerware, clay pipe, electrical porcelain, common-usage glass, cement, furnace refractories, and abrasives. Advanced ceramics are often cited as enabling technologies for advanced applications in fields such as aerospace, automotive, and electronics.

Advanced ceramic materials constitute an emerging technology with a very broad base of current and potential applications and an ever growing list of material compositions. Advanced ceramics are tailored to have premium properties through application of advanced materials science and technology to control composition and internal structure. Examples are silicon nitride, silicon carbide, toughened zirconia, aluminum nitride, carbon-fiber-reinforced glass ceramic, and high-temperature superconductors. Advanced ceramic materials, and in particular the structural segment of the industry, are the focus of this case study.

Industry Structure

According to Business Communications Company (BCC), a market research firm that covers the advanced ceramic industry, over 450 U.S. companies, including foreign-owned subsidiaries, are involved in the business of advanced ceramics. Of these 450 companies, approximately 125 produce structural ceramics. The size of these firms ranges from the small job shop to the large multinational corporation, and considerable variation exists among firms regarding their extent of manufacturing integration (Abraham 1996).

Current trends in this industry are for greater emphasis on the systems approach for the commercialization of new products. The systems approach comprises the full spectrum of activities necessary to produce the final system or subsystem, including production of raw materials, product design, manufacturing technology, component production, integration into the subsystem or system design, and final assembly.

The systems approach has resulted in new corporate relationships in the advanced ceramics industry. More consolidation of effort among companies is occurring because of the following factors:

(1) Complex technical requirements,
(2) High levels of sophistication needed to manufacture advanced ceramics,
(3) Advantages in pooling technology,
(4) Advantages in pooling personnel and company facilities, and
(5) Finite amounts of business that can support the companies in the industry.

Indications of this consolidation trend are the 180 acquisitions, mergers, joint ventures, and licensing arrangements identified by BCC from 1981 to 1995.

Research and development activities are carried out typically by large companies and institutions. However, a number of small start-up companies are also beginning to commercialize products.

Market Characteristics

Based on estimates from BCC, Table 9.2 summarizes the market size for the various advanced ceramic market segments in the United States. The total market value of U.S. advanced ceramic components for 1995 is estimated at $5.5 billion, and the market in the year 2000 is forecast to be $8.7 billion, for an average annual growth rate of 9.5 percent. Electronic ceramics has the largest share of this market in terms of sales—about 75 percent—although the structural ceramics market is substantial and is expected to experience rapid growth.

As seen from Table 9.2, the market for U.S. structural ceramics is expected to grow from $500 million in 1995 to $800 million by the year 2000, or at an average annual rate of growth of 9.9 percent. Such materials are used for high-performance applications in which a combination of properties, such as wear resistance, hardness, stiffness, corrosion resistance, and low density are important. Major market segments are cutting tools, wear parts, heat engines, energy and high-temperature applications, bioceramics, and aerospace and defense-related applications. The largest market share is for wear-resistant parts such as bearings, mechanical seals and valves, dies, guides and pulleys, liners, grinding media, and nozzles.

Table 9.2. U.S. Market for Advanced Ceramic Components

Market	1995 ($millions)	2000 ($millions)	Annual Growth Rate
Structural ceramics	$ 500	$ 800	9.9%
Electronic ceramics	4,215	6,573	9.3
Environmental ceramics	240	400	10.8
Ceramic coatings	575	940	10.2
Total	5,530	8,713	9.5

While the market for advanced ceramics is expected to grow significantly into the next century, certain technical and economic issues have to be resolved to realize this potential. Such issues include high cost, brittleness, need for increased reliability, repeatable production of flawless components and stringent processing requirements for pure and fine starting powders with tailored size distributions. The advanced ceramics market, and in particular the structural ceramics market, could grow even more if these problems could be overcome by industry. U.S. government agencies, including NIST, will continue to have significant roles in resolving these problems in order to assist U.S. companies in achieving early commercialization of innovative ceramics technologies.

ECONOMIC IMPACT ASSESSMENT

Based on initial interviews with industry representatives, firms in the advanced ceramics industry, broadly defined, appear to rely mainly on evaluated phase diagrams emanating from research conducted at NIST. If some had first relied on phase diagrams from alternative sources, then the production related efficiencies between the two groups could have been compared in order to ascertain a first-order measure of the value added attributable to the NIST-conducted research. Historically, all manufacturers in the industry appear to have had access to the *PDFC* volumes and have had such access for years. Hence, as with the other economic impact assessments conducted at NIST by the Program Office, a counterfactual evaluation method was used.

Based on information obtained from BCC and from NIST, a sample size of 32 advanced structural ceramics firms was identified for contact. This group is representative of the broader population of manufacturers of structural ceramics products that directly utilize, through the *PDFC* volumes, NIST's evaluated research. According to BCC, these 32 companies represent between 60 percent and 70 percent of the domestic structural ceramics industry as measured in terms of annual sales.

Representatives at NIST and at ACerS identified a contact individual in each company, and each individual was initially contacted to describe the purpose of the evaluation study and to solicit their participation. Twenty-eight of the 32 contacted individuals were eventually interviewed by telephone. The companies that participated in the interviews are listed, by name, in Table 9.3.

About one-half of the respondents followed the interview that had been sent to them prior to the actual telephone interview, and the rest preferred to discuss the role of evaluated phase diagrams in a more unstructured manner. This mix of response styles created difficulty in characterizing the qualitative observations of the survey in a statistical sense.

Table 9.3. Companies Participating in the Phase Equilibria Program Evaluation Study

Advanced Cerametrics	Engineered Ceramics
AlliedSignal	ESK Engineered Ceramics
AlSiMag Technical Ceramics	Ferro Corporation
APC International	Greenleaf Technical Ceramics
A.P. Green Refractories	Ispen Ceramics
Blasch Precision Ceramics	Kennametal
Ceradyne	Lucent Technologies
Ceramatec	Norton
Ceramco	PPG
Corning	3M
Delphi Energy and Engine Management System	Textron
Dow	Vesuvius
Du-Co Ceramics	WESGO
DuPont	Zircoa

In lieu of such a statistical analysis, several stylized facts about the general use of phase diagrams in the structural ceramics industry are noteworthy:

(1) Phase diagrams are used most frequently during the research stage of the product cycle; product design and development was the next most frequently mentioned stage for use,

(2) When queried about what action(s) would have been taken if appropriate evaluated phase diagrams were not available in the *PDFC* volumes, responses were varied but two opinions were consistently mentioned
   (a) search for non-evaluated equilibria data from other sources
   (b) perform internal experimentation to determine the appropriate phase relations,

(3) Regarding the perceived economic consequences associated with alternatives to the evaluated phase diagrams in the *PDFC* volumes, respondents were of the opinion uniformly that both certainty associated with the performance of the final product would decrease and the research or product design stage would lengthen by about six months, and

(4) While ceramics researchers generally have greater confidence in evaluated diagrams in comparison to non-evaluated diagrams, they scrutinize all phase

diagrams carefully in the area of interest on the diagram, whether it has been evaluated or not.

An estimate was made of the additional annual cost each company would incur in steady state for having to adjust to the counterfactual scenario in which no evaluated phase diagram information existed. These estimates were based on lengthy discussions with each of the company respondents about the cost of pursuing research projects in the absence of *PDFC* volumes and the frequency of such occurrences. In most cases, these estimates were formulated during the interview so the accuracy of the estimate could be scrutinized. The following situation typified the nature of these conversations:

> Company XYZ used the *PDFC* volume in about 40 percent of its research activity and product design and development activity. In the absence of such evaluated data, that is in the absence of any future research to evaluate phase diagrams at NIST, one to two additional person-years of effort would be needed each year to maintain the same quality of product and the same production schedule. Valuing a ceramics researcher at the fully-burdened rate of $200,000 per year, company XYZ would incur a permanent increase in costs of $300,000 ($200 *x* 1.5 person-years) to maintain the status quo.

Many respondents in small as well as large companies stated that, in all likelihood, their firms could not carry such additional costs. Therefore, quality, reliability, and new product introductions would fall.

Responses to the counterfactual scenario ranged from a low of $3,000 per year to a high of $1.7 million per year in additional labor and equipment costs. For 22 of the 28 companies that were willing to engage in this estimating exercise, the sum of the steady state additional annual costs is $6.467 million.

These 22 firms account for about 50 percent of the sales in the structural ceramics industry in 1997. Accordingly, the estimated sum of additional annual costs for the 22 companies has been extrapolated to the industry as a whole, and the sum is $12.934 million.

As an aside, based on information from the interview process, the 22 firms in the sample apply the *PDFC* volumes in a manner representative of the remaining firms that constitute the structural ceramics industry. Regardless of the size of the firm, phase diagrams are used in approximately the same product stages and with the same intensity. Also, regardless of firm size, typically only one or two engineers or scientists in each firm make use of the phase diagrams.

Analysis of Cost and Benefit Data

Table 9.4 shows the data used for the economic impact assessment. Research cost data come from Table 9.1. According to the management of the Phase Equilibria Program, the portion of research costs related specifically to advanced ceramics is inseparable from the total Program's research expenditures. Thus, these cost data include the costs of outputs beyond the scope of this case study. As such, the performance evaluation metrics that follow are biased downward.

The industrial benefit data are based on the 1997 point estimate of industrial benefits totaling $12.934 million. This estimate is extrapolated through 2001. This five-year projection time was not arbitrarily chosen. A number of respondents who had institutional knowledge about their company stated during the telephone interviews that their company's product mix would tend to change over the course of the next five to ten years. Thus, a five year projection seemed reasonable as the period during which individual benefits would be realized from NIST's investments in the recent six *PDFC* volumes relating to advanced ceramics (as discussed in the section about the Phase Equilibria Program). Annual industrial benefits were increased by an annual rate of 2.375 percent, the prevailing rate of inflation at the time of this case study.

Table 9.4. NIST Costs and Industrial Benefits for the Phase Equilibria Program

Year	NIST Costs	Industrial Benefits
1985	$420,000	
1986	420,000	
1987	382,000	
1988	294,000	
1989	255,000	
1990	265,000	
1991	87,000	
1992	94,000	
1993	103,000	
1994	105,000	
1995	97,000	
1996	136,000	
1997		$12,934,000
1998		13,241,000
1999		13,556,000
2000		13,878,000
2001		14,207,000

For evaluation purposes only, zero economic benefits have been assumed over the years 1985 through 1996. Obviously, this is an unrealistic assumption based not only on common sense but also on the survey responses. To illustrate, one survey respondent noted the recent use of *PDFC* volumes:

> Our company makes ceramic materials that are manufactured into wear resistant parts by our customers. The phase diagrams contain important information correlating melting points with the wear resistant properties.

Our research began in 1991, the prototype appeared in 1992, and the product was introduced in 1993.

However, no quantifiable information emerged from the survey interviews to facilitate an estimate of benefits prior to 1997. The omission of these pre-1997 benefits provides yet a second downward bias in the performance evaluation metrics.

Performance Evaluation Metrics

Table 9.5 summarizes the value of the three NIST performance evaluation metrics, discussed in Chapter 4, using a discount rate equal to 7 percent plus the average annual rate of inflation from 1985 through 1996; 3.65 percent. Certainly, on the basis of these metrics NIST's phase equilibria research program is worthwhile.

Table 9.5. Phase Equilibria Program Performance Evaluation Metrics

Performance Evaluation Metric	Estimate (rounded)
Internal rate of return	33%
Implied rate of return	27%
Ratio of benefits-to-costs	9

CONCLUSIONS

The counterfactual experiment used in this case study showed that, without NIST's research investments, ceramic manufacturers collectively would be less efficient in attaining comparable technical data. Ceramists would incur greater costs for internal research and experimentation. These additional costs would likely be passed on to downstream manufacturers and ultimately on to consumers of ceramic-based products. Thinking back to the discussion in Chapter 3, where we introduced the concept of counterfactual research investments to preserve the stream of returns generated by public investments, we see here a case where the counterfactual costs entail additional trial and error experimentation and literature search contemporaneous with product development, raising production costs of customized products and hence changing prices. Further, as a practical matter, even pre-innovation extra private research and technology development costs are likely to be reflected in post-innovation prices, and as a result the streams of economic surplus would typically be less than was the case with the provision of appropriate infrastructure technology with public investments.

10 ALTERNATIVE REFRIGERANT RESEARCH PROGRAM*

INTRODUCTION

The National Institute of Standards and Technology (NIST) is often called upon to contribute specialized research or technical advice to initiatives of national importance. The U.S. response to the international environmental problem of ozone depletion required such a contribution.

Historically, chemical compounds known as chlorofluorocarbons (CFCs) have been used extensively as aerosol propellants, refrigerants, solvents, and industrial foam blowing agents. Refrigerants are chemicals used in various machines, such as air conditioning systems, that carry energy from one place to another. Until the past decade, most refrigerants used throughout the world were made of CFCs because of their desirable physical and economic properties. However, research has shown that the release of CFCs into the atmosphere can possibly damage the ozone layer of the earth. In response to these findings, international legislation was drafted that resulted in the signing of the Montreal Protocol in 1987, a global agreement to phase out the production and use of CFCs and replace them with other compounds that would have a lesser impact on the environment.

In order to meet the phase-out schedule in the Protocol, research was needed to develop new types of refrigerants, called alternative refrigerants, that would retain the desirable physical properties of CFCs, but would pose little or no threat to the ozone layer. Possible candidates for replacement must have a number of properties and meet a number of criteria to be judged as feasible replacements.

Since 1987, the United States and other nations have forged international environmental protection agreements in an effort to replace CFCs with alternative, more environmentally neutral chemical compounds in order to meet the timetable imposed by the Protocol. NIST's research in this area is the focus of this case study.

---

* This chapter was co-authored with Matthew T. Shedlick. See Shedlick, Link, and Scott (1998).

NIST RESEARCH RELATED TO ALTERNATIVE REFRIGERANTS

NIST became involved in alternative refrigerant research in 1982 and has continued to support U.S. industry in its development and use of CFC replacements. The Physical and Chemical Properties Division of NIST's Chemical Science and Technology Laboratory (CSTL) has been the focal point for this research effort.

The Physical and Chemical Properties Division has more than 40 years of experience in the measurement and modeling of the thermophysical properties of fluids. The Division has been involved with refrigerants for about a decade. Early work was performed at NIST in conjunction with the Building Environment Division, and this work led to the development of early computer models of refrigerant behavior. In addition, research performed by Division members serves as a basis for updating tables and charts in reference volumes for the refrigeration industry.

Research on alternative refrigerants falls broadly into three areas:

(1) Effects of man-made chemicals on the atmosphere,
(2) Chemical and physical properties of alternative refrigerants, and
(3) Methods to place chemicals in machines.

The first area is referred to by NIST scientists as "understanding the problem," and the other two areas are referred to as "solving the problem." The primary focus of the Physical and Chemical Properties Division is on the properties of refrigerants.

The results from NIST's properties research were made available to industry in various forms. The most effective form for dissemination of information has been through the REFPROP program, a computer package that is available through NIST's Standard Reference Data Program. The REFPROP program is used by both manufacturers and users of alternative refrigerants in their respective manufacturing processes. A particular benefit of the REFPROP program is its ability to model the behavior of various refrigerant mixtures, and this has proven to be a key method in developing CFC replacements. The economic benefits associated with this program are specifically evaluated herein.

NIST's research efforts on characterizing the chemical properties of alternative refrigerants and how these refrigerants perform when mixed with other refrigerants potentially averted a very costly economic disruption to a number of industries. According to interviews with industry and university researchers, NIST served critical functions that were important to the timely, efficient implementation of the Montreal Protocol. Arnold Braswell (1989), President of the Air Conditioning and Refrigeration Institute, noted before Congress:

> Under normal circumstances our industry could do the necessary research and testing without any assistance, with equipment manufacturers and refrigerant producers working together. But there is too much to be done in a short time, to test and prove all of the candidate refrigerants, select the most suitable and efficient ones for various applications, design and test new equipment, and retool for production. This process takes time –

and money. Depending on the type of equipment, normally it would take 5-10 years, even after a refrigerant is available, to make appropriate design changes and thoroughly field test a new product before it is introduced commercially.

TECHNICAL OVERVIEW OF ALTERNATIVE REFRIGERANTS

Refrigeration

Refrigeration is a process by which a substance is cooled below the temperature of its surroundings. Objects can be cooled as well as areas and spaces. The type of refrigeration that relates to the research at NIST is mechanical refrigeration, as opposed to natural refrigeration.

A number of components are required for mechanical refrigeration. The vapor compression cycle of refrigeration requires the use of a compressor, a condenser, a storage tank, a throttling valve, and an evaporator. These elements, when working together, produce the desired cooling effect. The refrigerant is sent through the compressor, which raises its pressure and temperature. The refrigerant then moves into the condenser, where its heat is released into the environment, then through the throttling valve and into the evaporator where its pressure and temperature drop. At this point, the cycle begins again. The conduit for this heat exchange is the refrigerant.

For a refrigerant to be effective, it must satisfy the properties that are listed (not in any order of priority) in Table 10.1. Not every refrigerant meets these criteria. When deciding upon a refrigerant, all properties must be evaluated. For example, a refrigerant that has acceptable thermodynamic properties might be extremely toxic to humans, while one that is non-toxic might be unstable and break down inside the refrigeration machinery.

Chlorofluorocarbons

During most of the history of mechanical refrigeration, CFCs have been the most widely used refrigerants. The term chlorofluorocarbons refers to a family of chemicals whose molecular structures are composed of chlorine (Cl), fluorine (F), and carbon (C) atoms. Their popularity as refrigerants has been in no small part because of their desirable thermal properties as well as their molecular stability.

Chlorofluorocarbons have a nomenclature that describes the molecular structure of the CFC. In order to determine the structure of CFC-11, for example, one takes the number (11) and adds 90 to it. The sum is 101. The first digit of the sum indicates the number of carbon atoms in the molecule, the second digit the number of hydrogen atoms, and the third digit the number of fluorine atoms. Any further spaces left in the molecule are filled with chlorine atoms. Of the various chlorofluorocarbons available, CFC-11, CFC-12, and CFC-13 have been used most extensively because of their desirable properties. CFC-11 and CFC-12 are used in refrigeration and foam insulation. CFC-13 is a solvent used as a cleaning agent for electronics and a degreaser for metals. Listed in Table 10.2 are the various applications of CFCs, and it is important to note that refrigerants are only one-fourth of the applications.

Table 10.1. Refrigerant Properties

Chemical Properties
- stable and inert

Health, Safety and Environmental Properties
- non-toxic
- nonflammable
- non-degrading to the atmosphere

Thermal Properties
- appropriate critical point and boiling point temperatures
- low vapor heat capacity
- low viscosity
- high thermal conductivity

Miscellaneous Properties
- satisfactory oil solubility
- high dielectric strength of vapor
- low freezing point
- reasonable containment materials
- easy leak detection
- low cost

Table 10.2. Applications of CFCs

Application	Frequency of Use
Solvents	26.0%
Refrigeration, air conditioning	25.0
Rigid foam	19.0
Fire extinguishing	12.0
Flexible foams	5.0
Other	13.0

Ozone

The link between chlorofluorocarbons and ozone depletion has been debated for decades. Much of the impetus for international environmental treaties, such as the Montreal Protocol and legislation such as the Clean Air Act, has come from studies that assert that CFCs released into the atmosphere react with the earth's ozone layer and eventually destroy it.

The chemistry advanced by these studies suggests that once a CFC molecule drifts into the upper atmosphere, it is broken apart by ultraviolet light. This process releases a chlorine atom, which reacts with an ozone molecule. The reaction produces a chlorine monoxide molecule and an ordinary molecule, neither of which absorb ultraviolet radiation. The chlorine monoxide molecule is then broken up by a free oxygen atom, and the original chlorine atom becomes available to react with more ozone (Cogan 1988).

CFC Replacements

Research on alternatives to CFCs has focused on finding refrigerants that will not affect the ozone layer directly—that is refrigerants that do not contain chlorine or refrigerants that, when released into the atmosphere, will break down before reaching the ozone layer.

Three types of CFC replacement now being used and being studied for additional future use are hydrochlorofluorocarbons (HCFCs), hydrofluorocarbons (HFCs), and their mixtures. HCFCs are similar to CFCs except that they contain one or more hydrogen atoms which are not present in CFC molecules. This addition of hydrogen makes these refrigerants more reactive in the atmosphere and so they are less likely to survive intact at higher altitudes. HFCs are similar to HCFCs except that HFCs do not contain chlorine atoms; they are more likely to break up in the lower atmosphere than are CFCs and if they or their degradation products do survive to rise into the higher atmosphere they contain no chlorine atoms. Existing phase-out schedules, discussed below, mandate replacing CFCs and eventually HCFCs. Even though HCFCs are being used as substitutes for CFCs in some cases, this is not a long-term solution.

The proposed phase-out schedules deal with production and not use. With recycling, a compound may remain in use long after it has been produced. However, if it is no longer in production there may be a strong economic incentive to substitute for it.

For those concerned with the environmental effects of refrigerants, the relevant metric is the Ozone Depletion Potential (ODP) ratio. A substance's ODP can be found by dividing the amount of ozone depletion brought about by 1 kg. of the substance by the amount of ozone depletion brought about by 1 kg. of CFC-11. In this manner, CFC-11 has an ODP of 1.0—a very high ratio compared to HCFCs with ratios near 0.1, and certainly to HFCs with ratios of 0.

OVERVIEW OF THE REFRIGERANT INDUSTRY

The Montreal Protocol

The primary reason for the refrigerant industry's switch from CFCs to alternative refrigerants was the issuance of the Montreal Protocol in 1987, and its subsequent amendments. The Protocol, formally known as "The Montreal Protocol on Substances that Deplete the Ozone Layer," is the primary international agreement providing for controls on the production and consumption of ozone-depleting substances such as CFCs, halons, and methyl bromide. The Montreal Protocol was adopted under the 1985 Vienna Convention for the Protection of the Ozone Layer, and became effective in 1989.

The Protocol outlines a phase-out period for substances such as CFCs. As of June 1994, 136 countries had signed the agreement, including nearly every industrialized nation.

Each year the Parties to the Protocol meet to review the terms of the agreement and to decide if more actions are needed. In some cases, they update and amend the Protocol. Such amendments were added in 1990 and 1992, the London Amendment and the Copenhagen Amendment respectively. These amendments together accelerated the phase-out of controlled substances, added new controls on other substances such as HCFCs, and developed financial assistance programs for developing countries.

The main thrust of the original Protocol was to delineate a specific phase-out period for "controlled substances" such as CFCs and halons. For various CFCs, the original phase-out schedule called for production and consumption level to be capped at 100 percent of 1986 levels by 1990, with decreases to 80 percent by 1994, and to 50 percent by 1999. The 1990 and 1992 amendments, and the U.S. Clean Air Act amendments of 1990, called for an increase in the phase-out so that no CFCs could be produced after 1996. The Copenhagen Amendment called for decreases in HCFCs and for zero production by 2030.

Industry Structure

The alternative refrigerant industry consists of two types of companies: refrigerant manufacturers that produce the alternative refrigerants; and heating, ventilating, and air conditioning (HVAC) equipment manufacturers in whose machines the alternative refrigerants are used. These are the two industry groups that are considered the first-level users of NIST's research.

Refrigerant Manufacturers

This industry group consists of firms that manufacture a wide range of chemicals, including alternative refrigerants. The six major manufacturers of alternative refrigerants are listed in Table 10.3, along with their fluorocarbon production capacity.

Most of these companies have purchased multiple versions of the REFPROP program since its inception, with DuPont leading all companies in that it has purchased 20 versions. The companies listed in Table 10.3 have utilized the infrastructure research that NIST has performed on alternative refrigerants for their own development of proprietary refrigerant products.

Table 10.3. Fluorocarbon Production Capacity

Manufacturer	1995 Capacity (millions of lbs./yr.)
DuPont	550.0
AlliedSignal	345.0
Elf Atochem	240.0
LaRoche	60.0
ICI Americas	40.0
Ausimont USA	25.0

Each of these firms markets its own brand of refrigerants. For example, DuPont's alternative refrigerants are sold under the Suva brand, while Elf Atochem sells the FX line, and AlliedSignal the AZ line.

Precise market shares of the alternative refrigerant market are not publicly available. However, since 1976 the world fluorocarbon industry has voluntarily reported to the accounting firm of Grant Thornton LLP the amount of fluorocarbons produced and sold annually. Although these aggregate data do not allow for the calculation of firm-specific market shares, they provide some indication of the leading producers in the world. Joining the six companies listed in Table 10.3 are Hoechst AG from Germany, the Japan Fluorocarbon Manufacturers Association, Rhône-Poulenc Chemicals, Ltd. from the United Kingdom, Société des Industries Chimiques du Nord de la Gréce, S.A. in Greece, and Solvay, S.A. in Belgium.

Collectively, the global industry is a primary beneficiary of the research that NIST has done in the area of alternative refrigerants. However, this case study focuses only on the five largest U.S. companies in Table 10.3 because Ausimont USA has never purchased a copy of REFPROF.

HVAC Equipment Manufacturers

Firms in the heating, ventilating, and air conditioning industry are primarily engaged in the manufacturing of commercial and industrial refrigeration and air conditioning equipment. Such equipment is used at the local supermarket, in office buildings, in shopping malls, and so on.

The major equipment manufacturers include Carrier, Trane, and York. Their 1994 workforce levels and sales levels are listed in Table 10.4. The structure of the HVAC industry has been constant for nearly 20 years, with only the number of firms changing slightly—730 firms in 1982 to 736 firms in 1987. (Hillstrom 1994). The largest seven firms have maintained just over a 70 percent market share.

Table 10.4. Major HVAC Equipment Manufacturers

Manufacturer	Workforce	Sales ($billions)
Carrier	28,000	$3.80
Trane	13,000	1.42
York International	11,500	1.60

There are many other smaller HVAC equipment manufacturers that have purchased the REFPROP programs. The companies that have purchased REFPROF include those in Table 10.4 along with Copeland, Thermo-King, and Tecumseh.

ECONOMIC IMPACT ASSESSMENT

To quantify the economic impacts associated with NIST's research program in alternative refrigerants, two groups of first-level users of NIST's research were surveyed. The first survey group consists of the five larger domestic manufacturers of alternative refrigerants listed in Table 10.3. This group represents about 90 percent of the industry as approximated by production capacity. The second survey group consists of the six major domestic users of refrigerants noted above. These users represent over 70 percent of the industry as approximated in terms of employment levels. However, because there was no information available as to how representative this total group of eleven companies is in terms of benefits received, no extrapolation of benefits from the sample to the entire industries was made.

Separate interview guides were prepared for the five manufacturers of refrigerants and the six users of refrigerants. Each company was interviewed regarding a counterfactual scenario: "Absent NIST's research activities, what would your estimate be of the additional person-years of research effort that you would have needed to achieve your current level of technical knowledge or ability, and how would these person-years of effort have been allocated over time?"

Manufacturers of Alternative Refrigerants

Each of the five manufacturers of alternative refrigerants stated, in retrospect, that they anticipated the passage of the Montreal Protocol and were generally supportive of it for environmental and health reasons. The larger companies, in the absence of NIST's materials properties database, would likely have responded to the Protocol by hiring additional research scientists and engineers to attempt to provide the materials characterization and analysis needed by their in-house alternative refrigerant research programs or through their participation in research consortia. The smaller companies among these five reported that they would have relied on others' (in the industry) research, and in the interim would have looked for alternative uses of the refrigerants they produced.

All of the manufacturers were aware of the research at NIST, and four of the five manufacturers purchased NIST's REFPROP when it was first available in 1990 and the fifth purchased it in 1992. All used the most recent version of REFPROP for verifying properties of new compounds, either to be made by the company for general sale or to be made by the company for a specific customer. Interestingly, every respondent noted that REFPROP was easy to use and that minimal learning costs were associated with incorporating the software into production.

Regarding the calculation of benefits from NIST's research program, each of the five firms responded in terms of the additional person-years of research effort, absent the NIST-conducted research program, that would have been needed since the Montreal Protocol to achieve the same level of technical knowledge about alternative refrigerants that they have now. Each respondent was asked the current value of a fully-burdened person-year of research and this value was then imputed to the annual estimate of additional research needs, by company. To these annual totals, by company, the respondents' estimates of the value of additional equipment were added, although these costs were minimal compared to labor costs. The aggregate annual benefits for this group of five manufacturers are in Table 10.5. It is notable that each company's estimated annual benefits began as early as 1989, shortly after the Montreal Protocol went into effect.

Table 10.5. Economic Benefits to Refrigerant Manufacturers

Year	Industrial Benefits
1989	$2,090,200
1990	1,125,100
1991	1,107,400
1992	536,600
1993	552,400
1994	569,100
1995	586,300
1996	603,900

Users of Alternative Refrigerants

The six users of refrigerants produced a variety of heating, cooling, and other refrigerant equipment. As a group, they, like the manufacturers, anticipated the Montreal Protocol, and like the manufacturers they did conduct investigations into equipment efficiencies and alternative lubricants needed in anticipation of new refrigerants. Interestingly, these investigations were not referred to under the title of research and development, but rather as "component development" or "advanced development" activities. Accordingly, it was not surprising to find that these companies were less familiar with NIST's underlying research program into alternative refrigerants than were the refrigerant manufacturers.

However, each company was familiar with NIST's REFPROP. REFPROP is important to refrigerant users because it assists them in verifying the properties of alternative refrigerants, especially new ones. As one survey respondent noted, were REFPROP not available:

> We would have been at the mercy of the [refrigerant] manufacturers to meet deadlines ... this would mean that to deliver equipment that met Montreal Protocol specifications we would have been less reliable.

The refrigerant users were asked a delimited counterfactual scenario question. Specifically, each interviewee was asked the additional number of person-years of effort that would have been needed, absent NIST's REFPROP, for them to achieve the same level of product reliability as they currently have. Five of the six companies were comfortable answering this question; the sixth company was not comfortable offering even a ranged response. But since this company did report positive benefits, the median response from the other five was imputed to it. The additional person-years of effort reported by the interviewees were generally described in terms of needing additional quality control engineers. As above, each person-year was valued in terms of the company's cost of a fully-burdened person-year, and additional equipment costs were considered when relevant; they were most relevant in the first year of reported benefits, 1990. See Table 10.6.

Table 10.6. Economic Benefits to Refrigerant Users

Year	Industrial Benefits
1990	$2,342,500
1991	550,600
1992	534,800
1993	519,200
1994	503,900
1995	489,200
1996	475,000

Economic Analysis

Table 10.7 reports total NIST expenditures on research along with the sum of industrial benefits from refrigerant manufacturers, Table 10.5, and refrigerant users,

Table 10.6. All relevant NIST expenditures occurred between 1987 and 1993. At the time that the benefit data were collected in 1997, the latest version of REFPROF available was Version 5.0, released in February 1996. No research conducted at NIST after 1993 would have been used in Version 4.0 which was released in November 1993. The versions on which industry benefits are based were Version 4.0 and earlier ones.

Table 10.7. NIST Alternative Refrigerants Research Costs and Industrial Benefits

Year	Research Expenditures	Industrial Benefits
1987	$ 68,000	
1988	75,000	
1989	345,000	$2,090,200
1990	490,000	3,467,600
1991	455,000	1,658,000
1992	830,000	1,071,400
1993	960,000	1,071,600
1994		1,073,000
1995		1,075,500
1996		1,078,900

Performance Evaluation Metrics

Table 10.8 summarizes the value of the three NIST performance evaluation metrics, discussed in Chapter 4, using a discount rate equal to 7 percent plus the average annual rate of inflation from 1987 through 1996; 3.62 percent. Certainly, on the basis of these metrics NIST's alternative refrigerants research program has been worthwhile.

Table 10.8. Alternative Refrigerants Performance Evaluation Metrics

Performance Evaluation Metric	Estimate (rounded)
Internal rate of return	435%
Implied rate of return	28%
Ratio of benefits-to-costs	4

CONCLUSIONS

The interviews conducted as part of this case study suggested that there were other economic benefits associated with NIST's research that were not quantitatively captured by the performance evaluation metrics in Table 10.8. First, transaction cost savings could be substantial. That is, in the absence of reliable data concerning the properties of alternative refrigerant compounds, firms designing refrigeration equipment would be forced to rely on less comprehensive, less accurate, and more heterogeneous properties data furnished by individual chemical producers. The costs of evaluating those data could be significant, especially for a new refrigerant, and could conceivably be incurred repeatedly by numerous equipment designers who doubted the performance claims of suppliers. The estimation of these costs could add substantially to the benefit stream emanating from NIST's investments.

A second source of additional economic benefits could be ascertained from estimates of energy cost efficiencies that would not have occurred absent NIST's efforts. Given the deadlines for CFC replacement imposed by international agreements, in the absence of NIST's efforts it is certainly possible that more poorly researched, less optimal refrigerants would have been adopted and energy efficiency of equipment utilizing these inferior chemicals would have been degraded.

A third benefit resulting from NIST's involvement in refrigerant research was that NIST provided a degree of standardization of results that might possibly not have existed had alternative refrigerant development been left to industry alone. This standardization served to reduce uncertainty about refrigerant properties, and it allowed refrigerant manufacturers and users to develop new products with the knowledge that the underlying data upon which they were basing their product designs were valid.

A final important benefit of NIST's research program is the avoidance of burdensome regulations and taxes that could have been imposed upon the refrigerant producing industry had NIST's research been performed for and funded by the industry itself. Congressional testimony from the late 1980s indicates quite clearly that many interest groups viewed the refrigerant manufacturers as the cause of the ozone depletion problem and thus did not embrace the prospect of these same manufacturers profiting from the government-mandated increase in demand for alternative refrigerants. NIST's involvement as a neutral third-party served to defuse this politically charged issue by removing from consideration the perceived exploitation of the market response to the Montreal Protocol by these manufacturers.

11 SPECTRAL IRRADIANCE STANDARDS

INTRODUCTION

The Radiometric Physics Division is one of eight divisions within the Physics Laboratory at the National Institute of Standards and Technology (NIST). It conducts research programs and associated activities to fulfill its primary goals, to:

(1) Develop, improve, and maintain the national standard and measurement techniques for radiation thermometry, spectroradiometry, photometry, and spectrophotometry,
(2) Disseminate these standards by providing measurement services to customers requiring calibrations of the highest accuracy, and
(3) Develop the scientific and technical basis for future measurement services by conducting fundamental and applied research.

Hence, the technical scope of the Division includes:

(1) National measurement scales,
(2) Calibration services, and
(3) Research.

Regarding national measurement scales, related programs and activities are focused to link all optical measurement to the International System of Units (SI) base units. The candela is the SI base unit for luminous intensity. Regarding calibration services, related programs and activities are focused on measuring spectral radiance and irradiance. Radiance is the amount of energy existing on a surface, and irradiance is the amount of energy incident on, or projected onto, a surface. Finally, the research programs and activities support measurement and calibration. All of these infrastructure services and underlying research support a number of industries, including the measurement equipment industry, the lighting manufacturing industry, and the photographic equipment industry.

This case study considers specifically the economic benefits to industry that result from NIST's investments in the development and dissemination of spectral irradiance calibration standards.

THE FASCAL LABORATORY

Operations of the Laboratory

The Radiometric Physics Division is organizationally divided into three groups, each managed by a group leader who reports to the Division Chief, and the Thermal Radiometry Group is one of these groups. An important project with this Group is the operation and maintenance of the Facility for Automated Spectral Calibration, also known as the FASCAL laboratory.

The FASCAL laboratory was built in 1975 at an approximate cost to NIST of $250,000. The facility was needed in order to automate spectral radiometric calibrations. More specifically, it was needed to calibrate the 1,000 watt quartz halogen tungsten lamp for industrial and other manufacturers. Prior to 1975, calibrations were done in a variety of facilities within various laboratories at NIST.

The annual net operating budget for the FASCAL laboratory has remained constant over time, consisting of approximately one professional and one technical person per year. In 1995, total labor costs, fully burdened, were $250,000. In addition, the laboratory spends an additional $25,000 per year on equipment replacement, repair, and maintenance. Thus, the 1995 cost to operate the FASCAL laboratory can be projected into the future by accounting for only inflationary cost increases.

Calibration services are provided to industrial manufacturers and others on a for-fee basis. Revenues in 1995 were $125,000 per year. Thus, NIST's net annual expenditures to operate and maintain the FASCAL laboratory were, in 1995, approximately $150,000. Halogen lamps are also sold by NIST through the FASCAL laboratory. These lamps are sold to industry and to others at cost—$8,000 each. Approximately 60 lamps are calibrated and sold each year. With or without NIST, industry would buy these lamps calibrated in another way, and their cost is then not part of the cost of the NIST program. Note, however, that for our counterfactual analysis, we do not net out the calibration service revenues, but use NIST's gross investment costs. Recall the evaluations of the Optical Detector Calibration Program in Chapter 6 and the Alternative Refrigerant Program in Chapter 10, where revenues from NIST's services were not netted out of research expenditures. We want to compare the real resource cost for NIST to do the research with what the cost for the private sector would have been without NIST. The social cost is the total NIST research cost, whether some of the costs are paid by the private firms or not. Further, the revenues generated by NIST's services reflect benefits from NIST's investments. Those benefits would, for example, be measured when computing the social rate of return in the Griliches/Mansfield and related models.

Users of the Laboratory

The three major industrial users of the FASCAL laboratory's calibration services are measurement equipment and other instrumentation manufacturers, lighting manufacturers, and photographic equipment manufacturers. These are sizable industries. In 1995, the value of shipments in the measurement equipment industry was approximately $10 billion, $4 billion for lighting, and $25 billion for photographic equipment manufacturers. The fourth major user of the laboratory is the military.

Measurement equipment manufacturers, such as Hoffman Engineering and RSI, rely on calibration services in order to produce measurement equipment for companies and institutions that need to make accurate radiometric measurement. As an example, lighting engineering companies rely on optical measuring machines to quantify the amount of energy at a particular point in space. When designing to specification the lighting of a new facility, and hence the energy usage of a new facility, assurances are needed by both parties that the amount of light specified to be on particular surfaces is in fact the amount of light delivered. That is, assurances are needed that the measurement equipment is accurate. The costs of inaccuracy include wasted resources—excess energy resources being allocated to facilities—or delays, retrofitting, and legal expenses resulting from lighting below specification.

Lighting manufacturers, such as Phillips and Osram Sylvania, require calibrations in order to assure their customers about lighting efficiencies and color. As an example, when an engineering design/construction firm is given lighting specifications, the contractor will purchase/specify lamps from lighting manufacturers to meet these specifications under the assumption that they are correctly calibrated. The costs of inaccuracy in this case relates to purchasing lighting that is inappropriate, too much or too little, for the task at hand. Again, resources are being misallocated.

Photographic equipment manufacturers, such as 3M and Kodak, must be able to provide customers accuracy regarding film speed, color response, paper uniformity, and camera exposure times. As an example, when customers purchase film of a given ASA speed from different companies, they want an assurance that their photographs will be correctly exposed regardless of the film manufacturer. The costs of inaccuracy relate to customer dissatisfaction and wasted resources if the film is improperly exposed.

Finally, the military relies on spectral irradiance standards when testing the accuracy of their tracking and surveillance systems. For example, the military pilots wear special goggles when flying at night. These goggles facilitate low light levels in the cockpit for low altitude surveillance. If a warning light comes on that is calibrated incorrectly the pilot will be momentarily blinded until the goggles re-adjust. Such a situation greatly increases the probability of an accident.

Table 11.1 shows that the majority of the FASCAL laboratory's time is allocated to providing services to the lighting and photographic industries. The category "other" primarily includes calibrations for other laboratories at NIST.

ECONOMIC IMPACT ASSESSMENT

Collection of Impact Data

After preliminary discussions with the group leader of the FASCAL laboratory, one individual within each of the four major users groups was identified as an information source regarding the economic role of the FASCAL laboratory and its calibration services. Based on discussions with these identified individuals, industry-specific interview formats were formulated. It was determined at this point that the military users would not be included in the data collection phase of the case study because they have captive customers and thus do not face the same market pressures as private sector manufacturers.

Table 11.1. Allocation of FASCAL Laboratory Time

User Industry	Time Allocated
Measurement equipment industry	10%
Lighting industry	30
Photographic equipment industry	30
Military	20
Other	10
Total	100%

The group leader of the FASCAL laboratory was asked to identify a representative sample of companies in each of the three industries and a contact person within each for participation in the case study. Nineteen companies were identified. Table 11.2 shows the distribution of these companies by user industry, and the percentage from each that agreed to participate in the survey study. Table 11.3 identifies the participating companies.

Table 11.2. Participants in the FASCAL Case Study, by User Industry

User Industry	Participants	Participation Rate
Measurement equipment industry	4 of 7 companies	57%
Lighting industry	5 of 7 companies	71
Photographic equipment industry	3 of 5 companies	60

Experts within the Radiometric Physics Division estimated the coverage ratios for the three user industry samples. The four companies in the measurement equipment industry represent about 10 percent of 1995 sales of the industry; the five lighting manufacturing companies represent about 80 percent of 1995 industry sales;

and the three companies in the photographic equipment industry represent about 60 percent of 1995 industry sales.

Survey Results

After discussing industry-specific issues and trends, each participant was asked to respond to a number of background statements using a response scale of 1 to 5, where 5 represents "strongly agree" and 1 represents "strongly disagree." Participants could respond with "no opinion," and if they did their response was not included in the summary values below.

Table 11.3. Participants in the FASCAL Case Study

Measurement Equipment Manufacturing Companies
Biospherical Instruments
Grasby Optronics
Hoffman Engineering
RSI
Lighting Manufacturing Companies
General Electric Company
Inchcape-ETL
Labsphere
Osram Sylvania
Phillips
Photographic Equipment Manufacturing Companies
3M
Eastman Kodak
Xerox

Two conclusions can be drawn from the survey background responses summarized in Table 11.4:

(1) There is strong agreement that the FASCAL laboratory's services are important to each of the companies and to the companies' industries, and
(2) There is strong disagreement that business could be conducted as usual within each of the companies or in their industries in the absence of the services provided by the FASCAL laboratory.

In an effort to obtain more specific information on why the FASCAL laboratory and its calibration work is important, the topic was discussed in detail with each participant from both an industry perspective and from a company perspective. Typical comments by participants, across industries, are:

> Traceability through the FASCAL laboratory gives you confidence in your data and it saves time arguing with customers so that productive work can be done.

And,

> The standards have a tremendous impact. ... They make products comparable on an international basis.

Table 11.4. Summary Responses to Background Statements for FASCAL Case Study

Background Statement	Mean Response	
The FASCAL laboratory's services are important to the U.S. _____ industry.	Measurement: Lighting: Photographic:	5.00 4.50 5.00
The FASCAL laboratory's services are important to my company.	Measurement: Lighting: Photographic:	5.00 4.75 4.67
Most _____ companies in the United States could conduct business as usual in the absence of the FASCAL laboratory.	Measurement: Lighting: Photographic:	2.00 2.00 2.00
My company could conduct business as usual in the absence of the FASCAL laboratory.	Measurement: Lighting: Photographic:	1.25 2.50 2.67

More quantitatively, when asked a counterfactual question about what each company would do in the absence of the FASCAL laboratory, the majority of the companies responded that they would rely on foreign laboratories for calibration services. Specifically, 75 percent of the respondents in the measurement equipment industry, 100 percent of the respondents in the lighting industry, and 66 percent of the respondents in the photographic equipment industry so responded.

Economic Benefits Associated with the FASCAL Laboratory

Two potential benefit areas were identified during the survey pre-test interviews. One area of potential benefits relates to the improvement of product quality because of traceability to a national standard. The second area relates to reduced transaction costs between manufacturers and their customers because of the existence of accepted calibration standards.

Interestingly, verifiability between buyers and sellers is not a new issue to the lighting industry. In the mid-1960s, lighting companies used their own standards to produce lamps, florescent lamps in particular. Because companies knew how their lamps compared to their competitors in terms of lumens, companies, in a sequential fashion, would tend to overstate their lumens in order to increase their sales. This so-called Great Lumen Race persisted for a number of years because there was no basic standard against which customers could verify products. Eventually, the Government Services Administration began to test lamps supplied on government contracts against the NIST standard. When companies realized that such monitoring was occurring, they voluntarily adjusted their manufacturing process to conform to the NIST standard.

Improvements in Product Quality

Each survey participant was asked, using the 5-point strongly agree to strongly disagree response scale, "In the absence of the FASCAL laboratory, industry customers would be forced to accept greater uncertainty in products." There was generally agreement to this statement about product quality. The mean response was 4.5 in the measurement equipment industry, 4.0 in the lighting industry, and 3.67 in the photographic equipment industry.

While improved quality has a definite economic benefit, discussions with each participant about the level of quality that would exist in the absence of the FASCAL laboratory, and the associated dollar value of the difference in improved product quality were beyond the scope of their expertise. In a few cases, this issue was discussed with the company's marketing expert, but no acceptable metric for quantifying this benefit dimension could be agreed upon. One respondent stated:

> Even with foreign laboratories, lack of accuracy would cost people in society hundreds of millions of dollars simply because users of my equipment would be making inaccurate environmental [in our case] forecasts.

And another respondent stated:

> If the FASCAL laboratory closed, our company would have to spend a lot more time trying to achieve the same level of accuracy that we now have.

Therefore, while product quality is certainly an industrial benefit, it is not quantified for the purposes of this case study.

Reduced Transaction Costs

Regarding the second benefit area, it is well established in both the theoretical and empirical literature that standards reduce transactions costs between buyers and sellers. In other words, measurement-related disputes are resolved more quickly when standards are in place. Given that the pre-test respondents identified reduced transaction costs as one of the two benefit areas, the following series of five questions was posed to each participant:

(1) Approximately, how many disputes occur per year with customers regarding the accuracy of your equipment?
(2) In your opinion, is this number less than it would be in the absence of NIST's spectral irradiance standard? If yes,
(3) Based on your experience in selling products that are not traceable to a national standard, approximately what would be the number of such disputes per year in the absence of the FASCAL laboratory?
(4) Approximately, how many person-days does it take to resolve such a dispute?
(5) Approximately, what is the cost to your company of a fully-burdened person-year?

Summary responses, by user industry, are in Table 11.5.

Several industry-specific patterns can be seen from the responses in Table 11.5, keeping in mind that each industry is not equally represented by the sample of companies surveyed. First, the incidence of disputes varies across industry from 2.3 per year in the measurement equipment industry to 15.7 per year in the photographic equipment industry. Second, there is widespread agreement that the spectral irradiance standard reduces the incidence of disputes between buyers and sellers of equipment. Third, the expected increase in the mean number of disputes from the current situation to the counterfactual situation of no FASCAL laboratory is variable, ranging from a 17-fold increase in the measurement equipment industry to a 2-fold increase in the photographic equipment industry. However, the expected number of disputes in the absence of the FASCAL laboratory is more similar across industries. And fourth, the time needed to resolve a measurement dispute over accuracy varies from 2.8 person-days per dispute in the lighting industry to 30 person-days per dispute in the photographic equipment industry.

Quantifiable Economic Benefits

The economic benefits quantified in this case study are the transaction costs savings associated with the FASCAL laboratory and the related spectral irradiance standards. For each industry, these transaction cost savings are calculated as the mean number of reduced disputes per year; times the mean number of person-days saved per dispute, times 2 to account for a similar saving on the part of the customer; times the mean cost of a person-day.

Table 11.5. Transaction Cost Savings for FASCAL Case Study

Survey Question	Measurement Equipment Industry	Lighting Industry	Photographic Equipment Industry
Mean number of disputes over accuracy?	2.3/yr.	6.3/yr.	15.7/yr.
Would disputes increase absent standard?	75% yes	100% yes	67% yes
Mean estimated number of disputes absent FASCAL laboratory?	39/yr.	21/yr.	32/yr.
Mean person-days to resolve a dispute?	8.8	2.8	30
Mean cost of a fully-burdened person-year?	$92,500	$156,000	$148,000

Table 11.6 shows the total transaction cost savings, by industrial user, for the sample of surveyed companies. Also in Table 11.6, the estimated transaction cost savings are extrapolated to the industry as a whole based on the sample coverage ratios. As shown, for 1995, total industry transaction cost savings equals $3.42 million.

Table 11.6. Estimated Annual Transaction Cost Savings for Industry for FASCAL Case Study

User Industry	Sample Cost Savings	Coverage Ratio	Industry Cost Savings
Measurement equipment industry	$239,000	10%	$2,390,000
Lighting industry	51,000	80	64,000
Photographic equipment industry	579,000	60	965,000
Total			$3,419,000

CONCLUSIONS

Benefit data were extremely limited in this case study. As such, the performance evaluation metrics that were calculated are also limited. Using 1995 data, total economic benefits are estimated at $3.42 million. Actual NIST operating costs are $275,000. However, these operating costs do not take into account the cost to build the FASCAL laboratory in 1975. That cost was \$250,000, or \$585,000 in 1995 inflation-adjusted dollars. Assuming that this capital equipment depreciates over 20 years, given annual new equipment purchases as accounted for in the operating cost estimate, then approximately \$29,250 needs to be added to the \$275,000 of operating costs to arrive at a reasonable cost estimate to compare to the benefit estimate of \$3.42 million. Hence, the relevant ratio of benefits-to-costs is just over 11-to-1.

Recalling the discussion in Chapter 3, the FASCAL case is one where judgment suggests that the private sector's counterfactual investment to replace completely NIST's FASCAL laboratory would not have been a feasible scenario, so instead we have estimated the transaction costs that industry has avoided because of the NIST technology. Those estimates are a conservative lower bound on the benefits because we have not attempted to quantify the loss in product quality given the counterfactual absence of NIST.

12 PRINTED WIRING BOARD RESEARCH JOINT VENTURE

INTRODUCTION

In April 1991, the Advanced Technology Program (ATP) announced that one of its initial eleven awards was to a joint venture led by the National Center for Manufacturing Sciences (NCMS) to research aspects of printed wiring board (PWB) interconnect systems. The ATP project description follows:

> Printed wiring boards (PWBs) are often overlooked in discussions of microchips and other advanced electronic components, but they form the backbone of virtually every electronic product, providing connections between individual electronic devices. Although to date PWB technology has kept pace with the increased speed and complexity of microelectronics, it is approaching fundamental limits in materials and processes that must be overcome if the U.S. industry is to maintain a competitive position. (The U.S. share of the $25 billion world market dropped from 42 to 29 percent in 3 years.) Four members of the NCMS consortium, AT&T, Texas Instruments, the Digital Equipment Corporation, and Hamilton Standard Interconnect, Inc., will work with the Sandia National Laboratories (U.S. Department of Energy) to develop a more consistent epoxy glass material with improved mechanical characteristics for PWBs, improved processes and process-control techniques to produce more reliable solder connections, improved methods and technologies for fine-line imaging on the boards, and a better technical understanding of the chemistry underlying key copper-plating processes. Nine hundred U.S. firms in the PWB industry could benefit.

Project length:	5 years
ATP funds:	$13,783K
Cost-shared funds (est.)	$14,674K
Total project funds (est.)	$28,457K

As discussed in Link (1997), the PWB Project was completed in April 1996. Actual ATP costs (pre-audited) amounted to $12.866 million over the five-year (statutory limit) funding period. Actual industry costs amounted to $13.693 million. During the project the U.S. Department of Energy added an additional $5.2 million. Thus, total project costs were $31.759 million.

OVERVIEW OF THE PRINTED WIRING BOARD INDUSTRY

Early History of the Industry

According to Flatt (1992), Paul Eisler, an Austrian scientist, is given credit for developing the first printed wiring board. After World War II he was working in England on a concept to replace radio tube wiring with something less bulky. What he developed is similar in concept to a single-sided printed wiring board.

A printed wiring board (PWB) or printed circuit board (PCB) is a device that provides electrical interconnections and a surface for mounting electrical components. While the term PWB is more technically correct because the board is not a circuit, the term PCB is more frequently used in the popular literature.

Based on Eisler's early work, single-sided boards were commercialized during the 1950s and 1960s, primarily in the United States. As the term suggests, a single-sided board has a conductive pattern on only one side. During the 1960s and 1970s, the technology was developed for plating copper on the walls of drilled holes in circuit boards. This advancement allowed manufacturers to produce double-sided boards with top and bottom circuitry interconnections through the holes. From the mid-1970s through the 1980s there was tremendous growth in the industry. In the same period, PWBs became more complex and dense, and multilayered boards were developed and commercialized. Today, about 66 percent of the domestic market is multilayered boards.

Trends in the Competitiveness of the PWB Industry

As shown in Table 12.1, the United States dominated the world PWB market in the early 1980s. However, Japan steadily gained market share from the United States. By 1985, the U.S. share of the world market was, for the first time, less than that of the rest of the world excluding Japan; and by 1987 Japan's world market share surpassed that of the United States and continued to grow until 1990. By 1994, the U.S. share of the world market was approximately equal to that of Japan, but considerably below the share of the rest of the world, which was nearly as large as the two combined. While there is no single event that explains the decline in U.S. market share, one very important factor, at least according to a member of the PWB Project team, has been "budget cut backs for R&D by OEMs because owners demanded higher short-term profits" which deteriorated the technology base of the industry. Original equipment manufacturers (OEMs) are manufacturers that produce PWBs for their own end-product use.

Table 12.1. World Market Share for Printed Wiring Boards

Year	United States	Japan	Others
1980	41%	20%	39%
1981	40	22	38
1982	39	23	38
1983	40	21	39
1984	42	24	34
1985	36	25	39
1986	34	32	34
1987	29	30	41
1988	28	27	45
1989	28	31	41
1990	26	35	39
1991	27	34	39
1992	29	31	40
1993	26	28	46
1994	26	26	48

In 1991, the Council on Competitiveness issued a report on American technological leadership. Motivated by evidence that technology has been the driving force for economic growth throughout American history, the report documented that as a result of intense international competition, America's technological leadership had eroded. In the report, U.S. technologies were characterized in one of four ways:

(1) Strong: meaning that U.S. industry is in a leading world position and is not in danger of losing that lead over the next five years.
(2) Competitive: meaning that U.S. industry is leading, but this position is not likely to be sustained over the next five years.
(3) Weak: meaning that U.S. industry is behind or likely to fall behind over the next five years.
(4) Losing Badly or Lost: meaning that U.S. industry is no longer a factor or is unlikely to have a presence in the world market over the next five years.

The 1991 Council on Competitiveness report characterized the U.S. PWB industry as "Losing Badly or Lost." However, in 1994, the Council updated its report and upgraded its assessment of the domestic industry to "Weak" in large part because of renewed R&D efforts by the industry.

Current State of the PWB Industry

Table 12.2 shows the value of U.S. PWB production from 1980 through 1994 based on data collected by the Institute for Interconnecting and Packaging Electronic Circuits (IPC 1992, 1995a). While losing ground in relative terms in the world market, the

PWB industry grew in absolute terms over these 15 years. In 1994, production in the domestic market was $6.43 billion, nearly 2.5 times the 1980 level, without adjusting for inflation, and approximately 1.5 in real dollars.

Table 12.2. Value of U.S. Production of PWBs

Year	Value ($millions)
1980	$2,603
1981	2,816
1982	2,924
1983	4,060
1984	4,943
1985	4,080
1986	4,033
1987	5,127
1988	5,941
1989	5,738
1990	5,432
1991	5,125
1992	5,302
1993	5,457
1994	6,425

There are two types of PWBs that account for the value of U.S. production shown in Table 12.2: rigid and flexible. Rigid PWBs are reinforced. For most panels, this reinforcement is woven glass. Rigid PWBs can be as thin as 2 mils or as thick as 500 mils. Generally, rigid boards are used in subassemblies that contain heavy components. Flexible PWBs do not have any woven glass reinforcement. This allows them to be flexible. These boards are normally made from thin film materials around 1 to 2 mils thick, typically from polyimide. As shown in Table 12.3, rigid boards account for the lion's share of the U.S. PWB market (IPC 1992, 1995a). In 1994, nearly 93 percent of the value of U.S. PWB production was attributable to rigid boards. Of that, approximately 66 percent was multilayer boards. Multilayer boards consist of alternating layers of conductor and insulating material bonded together. In comparison, single-sided boards have a conductive pattern on one side, while double-sides boards have conducting patterns on both.

Table 12.3. Value of U.S. Production of PWBs, by Market Type

Market Type	1991 ($billions)	1994 ($billions)	1999 est. ($billions)
Rigid	$4.76	$5.96	$8.06
Flexible	0.37	0.47	0.68

As shown in Table 12.4, Japan dominated the flexible PWB world market in 1994; but North America, the United States in particular, about equaled Japan in the rigid PWB market (IPC 1995b).

Table 12.4. 1994 World Production of PWBs, by Board Type

Region	Rigid	Flexible
Japan	27%	48%
Taiwan	6	-
China/Hong Kong	6	-
Rest of Asia	9	6
Germany	5	-
Rest of Europe	13	-
Europe	-	14
Africa/Mid-East	4	-
N. America	29	30
S. America	1	-
Rest of World	-	2
Total	100% or $21.2 billion	100% or $1.65 billion

There are eight distinct market segments for PWBs (IPC 1992):

(1) Automotive: engine and drive performance, convenience and safety, entertainment, and other applications for diagnostic display and security.
(2) Business/Retail: copy machines, word processors, cash registers, POS terminals, teaching machines, business calculators, gas pumps, and taxi meters.
(3) Communications: mobile radio, touch tone, portable communication, pagers, data transmissions, microwave relay, telecommunications and telephone switching equipment, and navigation instruments.
(4) Consumer Electronics: watches, clocks, portable calculators, musical instruments, electronic games, large appliances, microwave ovens, pinball/arcade games, TV/home entertainment, video records, smoke, and intrusion detection systems.
(5) Computer: mainframe computers, mini-computers, broad level processors, add-on memories, input devices, output devices, terminals, and printers.
(6) Government and Military/Aerospace: radar, guidance and control systems, communication and navigation, electronic warfare, ground support instrumentation, sonar ordinance, missiles, and satellite related systems.
(7) Industrial Electronics: machine and process control, production test measurement, material handling, machining equipment, pollution, energy and safety equipment, numerical control power controllers, sensors, and weighing equipment.
(8) Instrumentation: test and measurement equipment, medical instruments and medical testers, analytical nuclear instruments, lasers, scientific instruments, and implant devices.

As shown in Table 12.5, most U.S.-produced rigid and flexible PWBs are used in the computer market. Rigid boards are used more frequently in communication equipment than flexible boards, whereas military equipment utilizes relatively more flexible boards (IPC 1995b).

Table 12.5. 1994 U.S. PWB Production by Market Type and Market Segment

Segment	Rigid	Flexible
Automotive	12%	12%
Business/Retail	3	0
Communications	25	11
Consumer Electronics	4	3
Computer	35	45
Government and Military	7	20
Industrial Electronics	6	4
Instrumentation	9	4
Total	$5.96 billion	$470 million

PWB producers are divided into two general groups: manufacturers that produce PWBs for their own end-product use and manufacturers that produce boards for sale to others. Those in the first group are referred to as original equipment manufacturers (OEMs) or captives, and those in the second group are referred to as independents or merchants. As shown in Table 12.6, independents accounted for an increasing share of all PWBs in the United States (IPC 1992). Their share of the total domestic market for rigid and flexible PWBs increased from 40 percent in 1979 to 83 percent in 1994. In 1994, independents accounted for 93 percent of the rigid PWB market.

Table 12.6. Producers of PWBs, by Producer Type

Type	1979	1981	1991	1994
Independents	40%	47%	66%	83%
OEMs	60	53	34	17

Table 12.7 shows PWB sales for 1990 and 1995 of the ten major OEMs in 1990 (Flatt 1992). IBM's sales decreased during this period, but it sold its military division in the interim. AT&T's sales increased, but in 1996 the segment of AT&T that produced PWBs became Lucent Technologies. Lucent Technologies is now an independent producer. Digital's PWB segment in 1995 was Amp-Akso and so 1995 sales for Digital are noted as not applicable, *na.* Amp-Akso, also an independent producer, had sales in 1995 of $105 million. Hewlett-Packard and Unisys were no longer in the industry in 1995 and hence their 1995 sales are noted as $0. During this

period of time, the major OEMs were continuing to experience the market effects associated with their strategic decision to cut back on R&D, and in some cases eliminate it altogether.

Table 12.7. PWB Sales of Major OEMs in North America

Company	1990 ($millions)	1995 ($millions)
IBM	$418	$300
AT&T	195	300
GM Hughes/Delco	153	140
Digital (DEC)	125	*na*
Hewlett-Packard	68	0
Unisys	55	0
Texas Instruments	50	50
Raytheon	35	35
Rockwell	24	24
Thompson	24	24

In comparison to the information in Table 12.7 on OEMs, Table 12.8 shows that the major independents' sales have generally increased. As a whole, their sales increased at a double-digit annual rate of growth over the time period 1990 to 1995. The major independent shops do not conduct R&D, but they continued to enjoy increasing sales of their technically simple PWBs.

Table 12.8. PWB Sales of Major Independents in North America

Company	1990 ($millions)	1995 ($millions)
Hadco	$158	$258
Photocircuits	125	265
Diceon Electronics	113	*na*
Zycon	108	170
Circo Craft	84	135
Advance Circuits	83	153
Tyco	66	*na*
Tektronix	61	*na*
Sanmina	61	*na*
Continental Circuits	60	110

Independent manufacturers of PWBs, for the most part, are relatively small producers, as shown in Table 12.9. In both 1991 and in 1994, the vast majority of independent producers had less than $5 million in sales. The independents also appear to be declining in number, a drop caused by a sharp decline in the number of smaller producers. Whereas 33 companies had sales greater than $20 million in 1991 (with 16 of those having sales greater than $40 million) 50 companies had sales greater than $20 million in 1994 (with 18 of those having sales greater than $50 million and 5 of the 18 having sales greater than $100 million). But, the nearly 600 companies with less than $5 million in sales in 1991 had fallen to approximately 450 by 1994, and the declining trend is continuing.

Table 12.9. Number of Independent Manufacturers of PWBs

Sales	1991	1994
Over $20 million	33	50
$10 - $20 million	40	70
$5 to $10 million	60	100
Under $5 million	592	450+
Total	725	670+

PRINTED WIRING BOARD RESEARCH JOINT VENTURE

Roles and Relationships Among Members of the Joint Venture

Although Digital Equipment (DEC) was one of the companies involved in the original NCMS proposal to ATP, it participated in the project for only 18 months. Its decision to withdraw was, according to NCMS, strictly because of the financial condition of the corporation at that time. DEC's financial condition did not improve, ultimately leading to the closing and sale of its PWB facilities.

Three companies joined the joint venture to assume DEC's research responsibilities: AlliedSignal in 1993, and Hughes Electronics and IBM in 1994. Also, Sandia National Laboratories became involved in the joint venture during 1992, as anticipated when NCMS submitted its proposal to ATP for funding. Sandia subsequently obtained an additional $5.2 million from the Department of Energy to support the research effort of the joint venture. These membership changes are summarized in Table 12.10.

The PWB research joint venture can be described in economic terminology as a horizontal collaborative research arrangement. Economic theory predicts, and empirical studies to date support, that when horizontally-related companies form a joint venture, research efficiencies will be realized in large part because of the reduction of duplicative research and the sharing of research results. This was precisely the case here, as evidenced both by the quantitative estimates of cost savings reported by the members and by the case examples provided in support of the cost-savings estimates.

Table 12.10. Membership Changes in the PWB Research Joint Venture

Original Members, April 1991	1992	1993	1994	April 1996
AT&T	AT&T	AT&T	AT&T	AT&T
Digital Equipment	-	-	-	-
Hamilton Standard	Hamilton Standard	Hamilton Standard	Hamilton Standard	Hamilton Standard
Texas Instruments	Texas Instruments	Texas Instruments	Texas Instruments	Texas Instruments
-	-	AlliedSignal	AlliedSignal	AlliedSignal
-	Sandia	Sandia	Sandia	Sandia
-	-	-	Hughes Electronics	Hughes Electronics
-	-	-	IBM	IBM

AT&T, Hughes, IBM, and Texas Instruments were four of the leading domestic captive producers of PWBs when the project began; and they were also members of NCMS, the joint venture administrator. Although in the same broadly-defined industry (i.e., they are horizontally related), two of these companies, AT&T and IBM, were not direct competitors because their PWBs were produced for internal use in different applications. AT&T produced PWBs primarily for telecommunications applications while IBM's application areas ranged from laptop computers to mainframes. Although Hughes and Texas Instruments produced for different niche markets, they did compete with each other in some Department of Defense areas. No longer a producer, Hamilton Standard purchases boards to use in its production of engines and flight control electronics. AT&T and Texas Instruments are not involved in these latter two product areas. In contrast to all of the above companies, AlliedSignal is a major supplier of materials (e.g., glass cloth, laminates, resins, copper foil) to the PWB industry. In addition, it is a small-scale captive producer of multilayered PWBs. These member characteristics are summarized in Table 12.11; when a member is not a producer it is noted by *nap*.

Organizational Structure of the Joint Venture

A Steering Committee, with a senior technical representative from each of the participating organizations worked collectively to direct and control the four research teams to ensure that each was meeting the technical goals of the project. NCMS provided the program management, coordination, facilitation, and interface with ATP for the PWB project. NCMS coordinated and scheduled activities and provided the interface between the administrative functions of accounting, contracts, and legal activities related to intellectual property agreements.

Table 12.11. Characteristics of Members of the PWB Research Joint Venture

Member Company	Type of Producer	Primary Market Niche
AT&T	captive	telecommunications
Hamilton Standard	*nap*	aerospace
Texas Instruments	captive	computers
AlliedSignal	captive	defense
Sandia	*nap*	*nap*
Hughes Electronics	captive	computers
IBM	captive	computers

The joint venture was organized to "mimic a company with a chain of command," according to one member of the Steering Committee. As well, according to this member:

> If it was not organized this way then no one would be accountable. Most of the people had this project built into their performance review. If they failed on the project, then they failed at work. The structure also allowed ease of reporting. The information flowed up to the team leader as the focal point for information distribution. The team leader would then report to the Steering Committee of senior managers who were paying the bills.

The joint venture's research activities were divided into four components:

(1) Materials,
(2) Surface Finishes,
(3) Imaging, and
(4) Product (research not product development).

Prior to entering the 1990 General Competition, the members of the research joint venture conducted a systems analysis of the PWB manufacturing process and concluded that fundamental generic technology development was needed in these four components of the PWB business. Each component consisted of a combination of research areas which provided significant improvements to existing processes, and explored new technology to develop break-through advances in process capabilities.

A multi-company team of researchers was assigned to each of the four research components. The four research teams were involved in 62 separate tasks. Each team had specific research goals as noted in the following team descriptions:

(1) Materials Team: The majority of PWBs used today is made of epoxy glass combinations. The goal of the Materials Team was to develop a more consistent epoxy glass material with improved properties. The team was also to develop non-reinforced materials that exceeded the performance of epoxy materials at lower costs. Better performance included improved mechanical, thermal, and

electronic properties (e.g., higher frequency) to meet improved electrical performance standards.

(2) Surface Finishes Team: Soldering defects that occur during assembly require repair. The goal of the Surface Finishes Team was to develop test methods to use during fabrication to determine the effectiveness of various materials used during the soldering process and to develop alternative surface finishes. These test methods can be applied during fabrication to ensure the PWB meets assembly quality requirements.

(3) Imaging Team: The goal of the Imaging Team was to investigate and extend the limits of the imaging process to improve conductor yield, resolution, and dimensional uniformity.

(4) Product Team: Originally, this team was known as the chemical processing team. Its goal was to investigate the feasibility of additive copper plating and adhesion of copper to polymer layers. Based on input from the industry, its focus changed as did its name. The revised goal of the Product Team was to study all roadmaps and specification predictions and then update the other teams regarding what technological advances would be needed. Specifically, the goal was to develop high density interconnect structures.

Given the generic research agenda of the joint venture at the beginning of the project, the organizational structure conceptually seemed to be appropriate for the successful completion of all research activities. At the close of the project, this also appeared to be the case in the opinion of the members. As a member of the Steering Committee noted:

> There is better synergy when a management team directs the research rather than one company taking the lead. Members of the Steering Committee vote on membership changes, capital expenditures, licensing issues, patent disclosures and the like. As a result of this type of involvement, there are high-level champions in all member companies rather than in only one.

Technical Accomplishments

NCMS released a summary statement of the technical progress of the joint venture at the conclusion of the project. The PWB Research Joint Venture Project accomplished all of the originally proposed research goals and the project exceeded the original expectations of the members. Based on the NCMS summary and extensive telephone interviews with each team leader, the following major technical accomplishments at the end of the project have been identified.

Materials Team

The major technical accomplishments of the Materials Team were the following:

(1) Developed single-ply laminates that have resulted in cost savings to industry and in a change to military specifications that will now allow single-ply laminates.
(2) Developed new, dimensionally stable thin film material that has superior properties to any other material used by the industry. This material has resulted in a spin-off NCMS project to continue the development with the goal of commercialization by 1998.
(3) Identified multiple failure sources for "measling". Measling is the separation or delamination at the glass resin interface in a PWB. The findings revealed that PWBs were being rejected, but that the real source for the board's failure was not being correctly identified as a problem with the adhesion of resin to the glass.
(4) Completed an industry survey that led to the development of a Quality Function Deployment (QFD) model (discussed below). The model defines the specifications of the PWB technology considered most important to customers.
(5) Completed an evaluation (resulting in a database) of over 100 high performance laminates and other selected materials that offer significant potential for improving dimensional stability and plated through-hole (PTH) reliability. Revolutionary materials have also been identified that exhibit unique properties and potentially can eliminate the need for reinforced constructions.
(6) Developed a predictive mathematical model that allows the user to predict dimensional stability of various construction alternatives.
(7) Developed, with the Product Team, a finite element analysis model (FEM) that predicts PTH reliability.
(8) Developed low profile copper foil adhesion on laminate to the point where military specifications could be revised to allow lower adhesion for copper.
(9) Developed plasma monitoring tool.
(10) Filed patent disclosure for a Block Co-polymer replacement for brown/black/red oxide treatments for inner layer adhesion. This substitute will facilitate lower copper profiles and thinner materials.

Surface Finishes Team

The major technical accomplishments of the Surface Finishes Team were the following:

(1) Improved test methods that determine the effectiveness of various materials during the soldering process, concluding that one surface finish (imidazole) is applicable to multiple soldering applications.
(2) Commercialized imidazole through licensing the technology to Lea Ronal Chemical Company.
(3) Conducted survey of assembly shops to determine the parameters manufacturers monitor in order to make reliable solder interconnections.
(4) Evaluated numerous other surface finish alternatives, and presented data at the spring 1995 IPC Expo in San Jose; paper won the Best Paper Award at the conference.

(5) Filed three patent disclosures: A Solderability Test Using Capillary Flow, Solderability Enhancement of Copper through Chemical Etching, and A Chemical Coating on Copper Substrates with Solder Mask Applications.
(6) Facilitated the adoption of test vehicles developed by the team for development use, thus saving duplication of effort.

Imaging Team

The major technical accomplishments of the Imaging Team were the following:

(1) Developed and successfully demonstrated the process required to obtain greater than 98 percent yields for 3 mil line and space features. When the project began, the industry benchmark was a 30 percent yield. The team obtained over 50 percent yield for 2 mil line and space features; when the project began the industry benchmark yield was less than 10 percent.
(2) Developed and now routinely use test equipment and data processing software to evaluate fine-line conductor patterns for defect density, resolution limits, and dimensional uniformity.
(3) Applied for patent on conductor analysis technology and licensed the technology to a start-up company, Conductor Analysis Technologies, Inc. (CAT, Inc.), in Albuquerque, NM. CAT, Inc. now sells this evaluation service to the PWB industry. According to NCMS, it is highly unlikely that a private sector firm would have developed this technology outside of the joint venture. Thus, commercializing this technology through CAT, Inc. has benefited the entire industry.
(4) Evaluated new photoresist materials and processing equipment from industry providers, and designed new test patterns for the quantitative evaluation of resists and associated imaging processes.
(5) Developed and proved feasibility for a new photolithography tool named Magnified Image Projection Printing; this tool has the potential to provide a non-contact method of printing very fine features at high yields and thus has generated enough interest to form a spin-off non-ATP funded NCMS project to develop a full scale alpha tool. No results are yet available.

Product Team

The major technical accomplishments of the Product Team were the following:

(1) Developed revolutionary new interconnect structure called Multilayer Organic Interconnect Technology (MOIT), described as the next generation Surface Laminar Circuit (SLC) technology; demonstrated feasibility of MOIT on 1,000 input/output Ball Grid Array packages and test vehicles using mixed technologies, including flip-chip.

(2) Completed industry survey related to subtractive chemical processes, additive processes, and adhesion. The results of the survey showed that there was no industry interest in the research area; therefore new tasks were undertaken.
(3) Identified chemical properties to enhance the understanding of the adhesion of copper to the base material, magnetic-ion plating of metal conductive layers, and the development of PTH models and software that are very efficient and cost effective to run.
(4) Developed evolutionary test vehicles that simulate Personal Computer Micro Interface Card Adapter (PCMICA) and computer workstation products. These test vehicles have been used to speed the development of new materials, surface finishes, and imaging technology by other teams.
(5) Performed several small hole drilling studies and minimum plating requirement studies for PTHs.
(6) Delivered paper on a finite element analysis model (FEM), developed with the Materials Team, which won the Best Paper Award at the fall 1994 IPC meetings in Boston.

RESEARCH COST SAVINGS, EARLY PRODUCTIVITY GAINS, AND OTHER EFFECTS

Conceptual Approach to the Analysis

The conceptual approach to the assessment of early economic gains from this joint venture parallels the approach used by others in economic assessments of federally-supported R&D projects. Specifically, a counterfactual scenario survey experiment was conducted. Participants in the joint venture were asked to quantify a number of related metrics that compared the current end-of-project technological state to the technological state that would have existed at this time in the absence of ATP's financial support of the joint venture. Additional questions were also posed to each team leader in an effort to obtain insights about the results of the joint venture that affect the industry as a whole.

In a preliminary 1993 study (Link 1996b), it was determined that only 6.5 of the 29 then on-going tasks would have been started in the absence of the ATP award. At project end, there were 62 research tasks, and it was anticipated that, as previously noted, a portion would not have been started in the absence of ATP funding. Accordingly, a counterfactual experiment was designed to relate only to the subset of tasks that would have been started in the absence of ATP support. Prior to finalizing the survey (discussed below), each team leader was briefed about this study at the April 1996, end-of-project Steering Committee meeting. Because this study was begun at the end of the joint venture's research, team leaders volunteered to respond to a limited number of focused questions. It was therefore decided that the survey would emphasize only one quantifiable aggregate economic impact, namely the cost savings associated with the formation of the joint venture through ATP funding. This limited focus had both positive and negative aspects. On the positive side, it ensured participation in the economic analysis by all members of the joint venture. And, any end-of-study comparison of quantifiable impacts would therefore represent a conservative estimate of the actual net economic value of the joint venture to date. Furthermore, the focus, as explained in Chapter 3, will then answer the well-defined question of whether the public/private partnership was more or less efficient than would have been the case if the private sector had done the investment on its own. On the negative side, there were a number of technical accomplishments identified during the study that, in the opinion of the members, have the potential in time to generate large economic impacts to the PWB industry and to consumers of PWB-based products. No aggregate estimate of the potential value of these impacts was obtained; only examples of productivity impacts currently realized by several of the companies were documented. As explained in Chapter 3, we do not attempt to quantify the social rate of return in the sense of the Griliches/Mansfield and related models. Instead, we employ a counterfactual analysis to compare the relative efficiency of having public investment versus not having it. In contrast to the economic impact studies of infrastructure investments carried out by the laboratories at NIST, in the case studied here the public institution is not the principal performer in the innovative investment.

Methodology for Data Collection

The methodology used to collect information for this study was defined, in large part, by the members of the joint venture. In particular, members requested that the information collected first be screened by NCMS to ensure anonymity and confidentiality, and then only be provided for the study in aggregate form. Under this condition, all members of the PWB research joint venture were willing to participate in the study by completing a limited survey instrument and returning it directly to NCMS.

The survey instrument considered these related categories of direct impacts:

(1) Scale, Scope, and coordination efficiencies,
(2) Testing materials and machine time savings,
(3) Other research cost savings,
(4) Cycle-time efficiencies, and
(5) Productivity improvement in production;

and these two broad categories of indirect impacts:

(6) Technology transfers, and
(7) International competitiveness issues.

The focused survey findings were supplemented by selected open-ended comments offered on the survey instruments; by personal discussions with the team leaders and company representatives during the April 1996, Steering Committee meeting, and by follow-up telephone and electronic mail discussions with available members.

Survey Results: Two Snapshots in Time, 1993 and 1996

Each member of the PWB research joint venture was asked which of the 62 major research tasks in which they were involved would have been started by their company in the absence of the ATP-funded joint venture. Aggregate responses suggested that only one-half would have begun in the absence of ATP funding. The other one-half would not have been started either because of the cost of such research or the related risk. Those tasks that would not have been started without ATP funding include: development of alternative surface finishes, projection imaging evaluations, revolutionary test vehicle designs, plasma process monitoring equipment, PTH modeling software, and approximately 25 others. And, of those tasks that would have been started without ATP funding, the majority would have been delayed by at least one year for financial reasons.

Direct Impacts to Member Companies

Regarding the five categories of direct impacts:

(1) Scale, Scope. and Coordination Efficiencies: Estimated Work-Years Saved By Carrying Out the Research as a Joint Venture: Two years into the project, the members estimated a total of 79 work-years had been saved from avoiding redundant research, valued at more than $10 million. At the end of the project, the members estimated a total of 156 work-years had been saved. The total value of these work-years saved was estimated at $24.7 million. The estimated $24.7 million savings were based on the additional labor costs to the member companies to conduct the identified research tasks that would have been conducted in the absence of ATP funds, and complete them at the same technical level as currently exists. Examples of work-years saved from avoiding redundant research in carrying out the work of the imaging team were provided by a member of the Steering Committee:

> The universal test vehicle developed by the imaging team was the foundation for the co-development and sharing of research results. Two examples of this relate to the evaluation of etchers and the evaluation of photoresists. Regarding etchers, one of the member companies did the initial evaluation, Sandia did the validation, and other member companies implemented the findings. Similarly, individual companies evaluated selected photoresists and then shared their results with the others. All members benefited from this joint development and sharing by avoiding redundant research time and expenses.

(2) Testing Materials and Machine Time Savings: Two years into the project, the members estimated cost savings of over $2 million from non-labor research testing materials and research machine time saved. At the end of the project, the members estimated the total value of non-labor research testing materials and

machine time cost savings associated with the tasks that would have begun absent ATP funding to be over $3.3 million. Related to research testing materials savings, a member of the Steering Committee noted:

> Before the consortium, there was no central catalogue of all the base materials used to produce printed wiring boards. Now, the Materials Component of the PWB research joint venture has produced a complete database of PWB materials that includes data on composition, qualifications, properties, and processing information for the domestic rigid and microwave materials. The information in this catalogue has saved research testing materials and will make it easier for designers and fabricators to select materials without having to search through supplier literature.

This member went on to note:

> Considerable problems were encountered in creating the database because (a) materials suppliers do not provide standardized property test data; (b) all of the data needed to process the material were not readily available; and (c) some of the test data appeared to be exaggerated. The database is presently available within the consortium and there are plans to make the database available to the entire industry over the Internet.

(3) Other Research Cost Savings: In the 1993 study (Link 1996b), members were asked a catch-all question related to all other research cost savings associated with the research areas that would have been started in the absence of ATP funds, excluding labor and research testing material and machine time. In 1993, these other cost savings totaled $1.5 million. In the 1996 survey, the same catch-all question was asked, and members' responses totaled over $7.5 million.

Therefore, the total quantifiable research cost savings attributable to ATP funds and the formation of the joint venture were, at the end of the project, $35.5 million—$24.7 million in work-years saved, $3.3 million in testing material and machine time saved, and $7.5 million in other research cost savings. In other words, members of the joint venture report that they would have spent collectively an additional $35.5 million in research costs for a total of $67.3 million—that is, in addition to the $13.7 million that they did spend, the $12.9 million allocated by ATP, and the $5.2 million allocated by the Department of Energy—to complete the identified subset of research tasks that would have been conducted in the absence of the ATP-funded joint venture at the same technical level that currently exists.

(4) Cycle-Time Efficiencies: Shortened Time to Put New Procedures and Processes into Practice: Two years into the project, the members estimated that shortened time to put new procedures and processes into research practice was realized from about 30 percent of the tasks, and the average time saved per research task was

nearly 13 months. At the end of the project, the members estimated that shortened time to practice was realized in about 80 percent of the research tasks that would have been started in the absence of ATP funds, and the average time saved per task was 11 months. Members did not quantify the research cost savings or the potential revenue gains associated with shortened time to practice. As an example of shortened time to put new procedures and processes into practice, a member of the Steering Committee noted:

> The use of the AT&T image analysis tool and the improvements made in the tool during the contract has made a significant reduction in the evaluation time needed for photoresist process capability studies. This reduction has occurred due to the improved test methodology and the significant improvements in the speed and accuracy now available in making photoresist analysis.

(5) Productivity Improvement in Production: Two years into the project, members of the Steering Committee estimated that participants in the project had realized productivity gains or efficiency improvements in production that could be directly traced to about 20 percent of the 29 research areas. The then-to-date production cost savings totaled about $1 million. At the end of the project, the members estimated productivity gains in production that could be directly traced to about 40 percent of the 62 research areas. The teams estimated the value of these productivity improvements in production, to date, to be just over $5 million. And, because the PWB research joint venture's research has just completed, future productivity gains will, in the opinion of some team leaders, increase exponentially. One example of productivity improvements in production relates to converting from two sheets of thin B-stage laminate to one sheet of thicker B-stage laminate. One member of the Steering Committee noted:

> For a business like ours, the cost saving potential was enormous. The problem was that reducing the ply count in a board carried risk: drill wander, reliability, thickness control, dimensional stability, and supply. The consortium provided the resources to attack and solve each of these problems. The result was that we were able to quickly convert all production to thicker B-stage, saving at least $3 million per year. Without the consortium this conversion might not have occurred at all.

Indirect Impacts on Member Companies and the PWB Industry

Two categories of indirect impacts were identified which already are extending beyond the member companies to the entire industry: advanced scientific knowledge important to making PWBs and improvements in international competitiveness. For these impacts, descriptive information was collected to illustrate the breadth of the impacts, but no effort was made to place an aggregate dollar value on them or to segment them by tasks that would and would not have been started in the absence of ATP funding.

This approach was based on the advice of the Steering Committee that attempting aggregate dollar valuations at this time would be extremely speculative in nature.

(6) Technology Transfer to Firms Outside the Joint Venture: Two years into the project, the members estimated that 12 research papers had been presented to various industry groups; 40 professional conferences fundamental to the research of the joint venture were attended; information from the research tasks was shared with about 30 percent of the industry supplying parts and materials to the PWB industry; and personal interactions had occurred between members of the Imaging Team and suppliers of resist to the industry. At the end of the project, a total of 214 papers had been presented related to the research findings from the PWB project, 96 at professional conferences and 118 at informal gatherings of PWB suppliers and at other forums. Additional papers were scheduled at the time of the study for presentation throughout the year. Members of the joint venture offered the opinion that such transfers of scientific information benefited the PWB industry as a whole by informing other producers of new production processes. They also benefited the university research community as indirectly evidenced by the fact that these papers are being referenced in academic manuscripts. Members of the Materials Team attended 10 conferences at which they interacted with a significant portion of the supplying industry. Specifically, they estimated that they interacted about the PWB project with 100 percent of the glass/resin/copper suppliers, 100 percent of the flex laminators and microwave laminators, 90 percent of the rigid laminators, and 50 percent of the weavers. Members of the Steering Committee were asked to comment on the usefulness, as of the end of the project, of these technology transfer efforts. All members agreed that it was premature, even at the end of the project, to attempt to estimate in dollar terms the value to the industry of these knowledge spillover benefits. While all thought that they were important to the industry, one member specifically commented:

> One indication of the successfulness of the technology transfer efforts can be reflected in the fact that two of the PWB program papers presented at the IPC conferences were selected as best papers at these conferences. The IPC conferences are recognized worldwide as the premier PWB industry conferences. I think this shows that the industry appreciated the depth of the technology effort. Another indication of the usefulness of the technology transfer process is the fact that new PWB manufacturers are exhibiting interest in joining two proposed follow-on programs to continue certain areas of the current research.

(7) International Competitiveness Issues: The health of the domestic PWB industry is fundamental to companies becoming more competitive in the world market. At a recent meeting, NCMS gave its collaborative project excellence award to the ATP-sponsored PWB project. At that meeting the NCMS president credited the project with saving the PWB industry in the U.S. with its approximately 200,000 jobs. As shown in Table 12.12, the members of the PWB Research Joint Venture

perceived that as a result of their involvement in the joint venture, their company has become more competitive in certain segments of the world market such as computing, the fastest growing market for PWBs. Although any one member company is involved in only one or two market segments, thus limiting the number of team members' responses relevant to each market segment, all members indicated that their companies' market shares either stayed the same or increased as a result of being involved in the PWB project. Likewise, as shown in Table 12.13, the members of the teams perceived that the domestic PWB industry as a whole has increased its competitive position in selected world markets as a result of the accomplishments of the joint venture. Most respondents expressed an opinion about the effects of the PWB Research Joint Venture on the industry share of the designated segments of the world PWB market. The responses indicate that the PWB project has increased industry's share in every market segment, with the most positive responses relating to the computer and military segments. No member was of the opinion that they or other members of the joint venture had increased their share at the expense of non-members because the results of the PWB project have been widely disseminated. In addition, some members of the Steering Committee felt that the research results from the PWB Research Joint Venture had the potential to enhance the international competitive position of the U.S. semiconductor industry. It was the opinion of one member that:

> Through this program, the PWB industry is learning to produce higher density PWBs with finer lines, reduced hole sizes, and new surface finishes. This is allowing the semiconductor industry to decrease the size of their component packages or eliminate them totally. This should have a pronounced effect on the competitiveness of the semiconductor industry in the future, although there is no evidence to date.

Summary and Interpretation of the Survey Results

ATP's funding of the PWB Research Joint Venture Project had a number of direct and indirect economic impacts. Of the direct impacts, the largest to date were in terms of R&D efficiency. The project achieved at least a 53 percent reduction in overall research costs from what the participants expected would have been spent if the research had been undertaken by the companies individually rather than by the PWB research joint venture. This increased research efficiency in turn has led to reduced cycle time for both new project development and new process development. Collectively, the impacts resulted in productivity improvements for member companies and improved competitive positions in the world market. Through the knowledge dissemination activities of members of the joint venture, the capabilities of the entire industry are improving. These technology advancements are thus improving the world market share and the competitive outlook of the U.S. PWB industry.

Table 12.12. Competitive Position of Member Companies in World PWB Market

As a result of my company's involvement in the PWB Research Joint Venture, my company's share of each of the following segments of the PWB market has ...
(increased=3; stayed the same=2; decreased=1; no opinion=0)

Market Segment	My company's market share has ...
Automotive	2.00 (n=1)
Communications	2.50 (n=4)
Consumer electronics	2.00 (n=1)
Computer and business equipment	2.67 (n=3)
Government and military	2.50 (n=4)
Industrial electronics	2.33 (n=3)
Instrumentation	2.00 (n=3)

n=number of respondents to the question.; mean response shown

Table 12.13. Competitive Position of the PWB Industry in the World PWB Market

I perceive that as a result of the accomplishments of the PWB Research Joint Venture, the PWB industry's share of each of the following segments of the PWB market has ...
(increased=3; stayed the same=2; decreased=1; no opinion=0)

Market Segment	World market share has ...
Automotive	2.20 (n=5)
Communications	2.67 (n=6)
Consumer electronics	2.60 (n=5)
Computer and business equipment	2.83 (n=6)
Government and military	3.00 (n=6)
Industrial electronics	2.50 (n=6)
Instrumentation	2.33 (n=6)

n=number of respondents to the question.; mean response shown

The survey findings associated with the above direct and indirect economic benefits are summarized in Table 12.14. Therein, the categories of direct economic impacts to member companies are separated into those for which dollar values were obtained and those for which dollar values were not obtained, so-called quantified and non-quantified economic impacts.

The survey results described in the previous sections and summarized in Table 12.14 should be interpreted as only partial and preliminary estimates of project impacts. First, although ATP funding of the joint venture has led directly to research cost savings and early production cost savings and quality improvements, the bulk of the production cost savings and performance gains will be realized in the future both in member companies and in other companies in the industry as the research results diffuse and are more widely implemented. As such, the valued economic impacts reported in Table 12.14 are a modest lower-bound estimate of the long-run economic benefits associated with ATP's funding of the joint venture research.

Table 12.14. Summary of PWB Survey Findings on Partial Early-Stage Economic Impacts

Categories of Impacts	After 2 Years	At End of Project
Direct impacts to member companies		
Quantified economic impacts		
Research cost savings		
Work-years saved	$10.0 million	$24.7 million
Testing materials and machine time saved	$ 2.0 million	$ 3.3 million
Other research cost savings	$ 1.5 million	$ 7.5 million
Production cost savings		
Productivity improvements	$ 1.0 million	$ 5.0 million
Non-quantified economic impacts		
Shortened time to practice		
Average time saved per research task	12.7 months	11.0 months
Indirect impacts on member companies		
Competitive position in world markets	increased	increased
Spillover impacts on PWB industry		
Technology transfer		
Research papers	12	214
Conferences attended	40	96
Competitive position in world markets	increased	increased

A limitation of the methodology is that the data collected represent opinions from participants rather than market determined economic outcomes from the research of the joint venture. The participants in the PWB Research Joint Venture are obviously those in the most informed position to discuss research cost savings, potential applications, and economic consequences from the results obtained; full impacts across the marketplace cannot be observed instantaneously at the end of the project, but only in the future as research results diffuse and become embodied in PWB products.

CONCLUSIONS

During the April 1996, Steering Committee meeting of the PWB Research Joint Venture, the members of the committee were asked to complete the following statement: *My company has benefited from its involvement in the PWB joint venture in such non-technical ways as...* Representative responses were:

> We have learned to work and be much more open with other industry members. We have learned where other companies stand on technology. We have learned we in the industry all have the same problems and can work together to solve them. We have learned how to work with the Federal Labs, something we have never done before.
>
> We have an increased awareness of industry trends, needs, and approaches. We have learned that our company's intellectual property is not as [difficult to protect] as we initially believed—rarely can it be directly applied by our industry colleagues.
>
> We have gained prestige from being associated with the program. The joint NCMS/NIST/ATP research program has a national recognition. Suppliers that would not normally participate in collaborative projects will when a team like this is formed to become a joint customer.

The foregoing responses reflect the PWB research joint venture participants' satisfaction with their successful cooperative efforts to create generic enabling technology that they expect to be instrumental in the competitive resurgence of the U.S. PWB industry. Our counterfactual analysis shows that for areas where independent private research would have occurred in the absence of the ATP-funded joint venture, the venture cut the cost of the new technologies roughly in half.

13 FLAT PANEL DISPLAY JOINT VENTURE

INTRODUCTION

According to a U.S. Department of Defense report (1993, p. 1):

> Flat panel displays represent a technological and business area of great concern worldwide. This is because these devices are recognized as the critical human interface device in many military and industrial systems and commercial products in an increasingly information intensive world.

Given this view, the wide-spread belief that flat panel displays (FPDs) will replace the cathode ray tube (CRT) in most American weapon systems before the turn of the century, and the realization that Japan's share of the world flat panel market dwarfed that of the United States and will likely continue to do so for at least the near term, it is not surprising that governmental support for the industry was forthcoming.

Government support took a number of forms. One form of direct support came in the form of a defense-oriented initiative. The National Flat Panel Display Initiative was announced in 1994. This program provided direct funding to the then very thin domestic flat panel industry. A second form of support came through a partnership between the Advanced Technology Program (ATP) within the U.S. Department of Commerce's National Institute of Standards and Technology (NIST) and a research joint venture of flat panel display manufacturers. A group of small, flat panel companies took the initiative to form a research joint venture and apply to the ATP's initial competition. And, the joint venture was one of the eleven initial competitors that received funding.

The ATP-funded initiative represents an industry-initiated effort to revive itself and to set in motion a research agenda that has the potential to begin to reposition U.S. firms in the international flat panel market. The qualitative evidence in this case study, based on Link (1998), provides an early-stage indication of the impact that the ATP program had on the venture and will likely have on industry in the future.

U.S. FLAT PANEL DISPLAY INDUSTRY AND TECHNOLOGY

Early Development of the Industry

Flat panel display (FPD) is a term that describes technology for displaying visual information in a package that has a depth significantly smaller than its horizontal or vertical dimensions. This technology was first developed in the United States at the University of Illinois in the early 1960s. Soon thereafter, RCA, Westinghouse, and General Electric were researching the feasibility of flat panels operating on liquid crystal technology. By the early 1970s, IBM was researching an alternative—plasma display technology. However, none of these companies continued their research in FPDs.

At RCA, flat panel technology was seen as a commercial alternative to the television cathode ray tube (CRT), but because RCA's management at that time viewed this technology as a threat to its existing business, flat panel technology was never exploited to its commercial potential. Research at Westinghouse successfully led to the development of active matrix liquid crystal displays and electroluminescent displays, but because of the company's weak position in the television market financial support for the development of prototypes was canceled. And similarly, changes in the corporate strategy at General Electric (e.g., the divestiture of their consumer electronics group in the early 1970s) effectively stopped the company's research related to FPDs. Finally, IBM, which had completed some pioneering research in plasma display technology and actually established and operated a plasma panel manufacturing plant for several years, became convinced that liquid crystal display technology was more promising. They divested their plasma operation, but were not able to find a U.S. partner for liquid crystal research.

In the late 1970s and early 1980s other domestic companies considered entering the FPD market, but none did because of the large minimum R&D and production commitment needed. These companies included Beckman Instruments, Fairchild, Hewlett-Packard, Motorola, Texas Instruments, and Timex.

Japanese companies, Sharp in particular, began to specialize in flat panels in the early 1970s in response to the demand for low-information content displays (e.g., watches and portable calculators). Research in Japan progressed rapidly, and by the mid-1980s a number of Japanese companies were producing portable television screens based on active matrix liquid crystal displays. By the end of the 1980s, aided in part by the investment support that the Japanese firms received from Ministry of International Trade and Industry (MITI), Japan had established itself as the world leader in flat panel technology.

The lack of presence of U.S. firms in the global flat panel display market is in part because of the difference between R&D and manufacturing (McLoughlin and Nunno 1995, p. 10):

> Several U.S. firms were early inventors and experimenters in FPD technologies and are superb at developing new FPD technologies. However, the U.S. commercial manufacturing base for FPD products is not as developed. A survey of U.S. firms which either closed or sold FPD production facilities prior to 1990 found several common reasons why these firms were no longer in the industry: the belief that advanced displays were not central to the firm's business strategy; the cost of capital for establishing an FPD manufacturing line; the fear that Japanese competition is too strong to overcome; and the belief that the global economy allows purchases of FPD technology from any source, domestic or foreign.

Flat Panel Display Technology

In the most general sense, a FPD consists of two glass plates with an electrically-optical material compressed between them. This sandwiched material responds to an electrical signal by reflecting or emitting light. On the glass plates are rows and columns of electrical conductors that form plates for a grid pattern, and it is the intersection of these rows and columns that define picture elements, called pixels. The modulation of light by each pixel creates the images on the screen.

There are three broad types of commercially available FPDs: liquid crystal displays, electroluminescent displays, and plasma display panels.

A liquid crystal display (LCD) consists of two flat glass substrates with a matrix of indium tin oxide on the inner surfaces and a polarized film on the outer surfaces. The substrates are separated by micron-sized spacers, the outer edges are sealed, and the inner void is filled with a liquid crystal fluid that changes the transmission of light coming through the plates in response to voltage applied to the cell. The light source for a LCD is generally a cathode, florescent, or halogen bulb placed behind the rear plate.

The most common flat panel display is a passive matrix LCD (PMLCD). These panels were first used in watches and portable calculators as early as the 1970s. Characteristic of PMLCDs are horizontal electrodes on one plate and vertical electrodes on the other plate. Each pixel is turned on and off as voltage passes across rows and columns. Although easy to produce, PMLCDs respond slowly to electrical signals and are thus unacceptable for video use.

Active matrix LCDs (AMLCDs) rely on rapidly-responding switching elements at each pixel (as opposed to one signal on the grid) to control the on-off state. This control is achieved by depositing at least one silicon transistor at each pixel on the inner surface of the rear glass. The advantages associated with AMLCDs are color quality and power efficiency, hence they are dominant in the notebook computer and pocket television markets. The disadvantages of AMLCDs is their small size and high cost.

Whereas LCDs respond to an external light source, electroluminescent displays (ELDs) generate their own light source. Sandwiched between the glass substrate electrodes is a solid phosphor material that glows when exposed to an electric current. The advantages of ELDs are that they are rugged, power efficient, bright, and can be produced in large sizes; but ELDs are in the development stage for color capabilities. ELDs are primarily used in industrial process control, military applications, medical and analytical equipment, and transportation.

Like ELDs, plasma display panels (PDPs) rely on emissive display technology. Phosphors are deposited on the front and back substrates of glass panels. In response to a plasma or florescent lamp, inert gas is discharged between the plates of each cell to generate light. While offering a wide viewing angle and being relatively inexpensive to produce, PDPs are not power efficient and their color brightness is inferior to that of LCDs for small displays. PDPs are used in industrial and commercial areas as multiviewer information screens and are being developed for HDTV.

Current Structure of the Industry

In the early 1990s, the demand for laptop computers increased dramatically. Then, U.S. producers of FPDs were small, research-based companies capable of only producing small volumes of low-information content displays. U.S. producers—Apple, Compaq, IBM, and Tandy in particular—were soon in a position of needing thousands of flat panels each month. However, the domestic FPD industry was unable to meet this demand or to increase its production capabilities rapidly. On July 18, 1990, in response to the huge increase in FPD imports, U.S. manufacturers filed an anti-dumping petition with the U.S. Department of Commerce's International Trade Administration (ITA) and with the International Trade Commission (ITC). While duties were placed on Japanese AMLCDs from 1991 to 1993, the end result of the anti-dumping case was not to bolster U.S. FPD manufacturers but rather to drive certain domestic manufacturers offshore.

In 1993, the National Economic Council (NEC) and President Clinton's Council of Economic Advisors concluded that the U.S. FPD industry illustrated the need for coordination between commercial- and defense-technology. As a result of a NEC-initiated study, the National Flat Panel Display Initiative was announced in April 1994. This initiative was, according to Flamm (1994, p. 27):

> A five-year, $587-million program to jump-start a commercial industrial base that will be able to meet DOD's needs in the next century.

Even with the National Flat Panel Display Initiative, U.S. flat panel producers are clearly a minor player in the global market (Krishna and Thursby 1996). Table 13.1 shows the size of the world FPD market beginning in 1983, with projections to 2001. Noticeable in Table 13.1 is the greater than 10-fold increase in the nominal value of shipments between 1985 and 1986 in large part because of the successful introduction of a variety of new electronic products into the market by the Japanese. Table 13.2 shows the distribution of shipments by technology for 1993, with projections to 2000. Clearly, LCDs dominated the world market in 1993 as they do now, with the greatest future growth expected in AMLCDs. Finally, Table 13.3 shows the 1993 world market shares (based on production volume) for Japan and the United States, by technology. According to Hess (1994), the Japanese company Sharp held in 1994 over 40 percent of the world market for flat panels.

Table 13.1. World Flat Panel Display Market

Year	Value of Shipments ($billions)
1983	$ 0.05
1984	0.08
1985	0.12
1986	1.66
1987	2.03
1988	2.58
1989	3.23
1990	4.44
1991	4.91
1992	5.51
1993	7.14
1994	9.33
1995	11.50
1996 (est.)	13.04
1997 (est.)	14.55
1998 (est.)	16.12
1999 (est.)	17.73
2000 (est.)	19.51
2001 (est.)	22.46

Table 13.2. Distribution of World FPD Shipments, by Technology

Technology	1993	2000 (est.)
Non-emissive (LDC)	87%	89%
AMLCD	29	55
PMLCD and other	58	34
Emissive	13	11
Plasma	4	4
Electroluminescent	1	2
Others	8	5

ATP-FUNDED FLAT PANEL DISPLAY JOINT VENTURE

ATP Award to the Flat Panel Display Joint Venture

In April 1991, ATP announced that one of its initial eleven competitive awards was to a joint venture managed by the American Display Consortium (ADC) to advance and strengthen the basic materials and manufacturing process technologies needed for U.S. flat panel manufacturers to become world class producers of low-cost, high-volume, state-of-the-art advanced display products. The initial ATP press release of the five-year $15 million project was as follows:

> The trend in the multi-billion-dollar display industry for computers, televisions, and other commercially important products is toward larger and higher-resolution "flat panel" displays. Beyond the development of the display itself, successful commercialization of low-cost, high-quality flat panel displays will require important advances in testing and repair equipment, as well as better connection and packaging technologies. ADC, a joint venture of relatively small U.S. producers of flat panel displays, proposes a linked series of research programs to develop automated inspection and repair technology essential to large-volume production of these displays and advance two generic technologies for interconnections (the electronic links between the display panel and the microchips that drive the displays) and packaging: "flip chip-on-glass" (FCOG) and silicon ICs-on-glass (SOG). The results will be applicable to the design, production, testing, and manufacture of any of the several different types of flat panel displays. The two companies that direct the major research tasks in this project are Photonics Imaging (Northwood, Ohio), and Planar Systems, Inc. (Beaverton, Ore.). Seven other companies also will participate.
>
> ATP Award: $7,305 K
> Total Project Budget: $14,909 K

The project was completed in August 1996. Total project costs amounted to $14,910 K. Actual ATP costs (pre-audit) amounted to $7,306 K over the five-year (statutory limit) funding period; actual industry costs amounted to $7,604 K.

Table 13.3. 1993 World FPD Market Shares, by Country

Country	LCD	AMLCD	Plasma	Electroluminescent
Japan	92%	98%	68%	47%
United States	1	1	19	50
Others	7	1	13	3

Both of the lead companies are relatively small. The larger of the two is Planar Systems, Inc. Planar is a public company, and it is the leading domestic developer, manufacturer, and marketer of high performance electronic display products. Its technological base is electroluminescent technology. Photonics Imaging is a very small investor-owned research company. Its expertise relates to control technology as applied to automation of the production process. The other companies are small and had minor roles.

The primary motivations for these two companies to organize under the umbrella of the American Display Consortium were two. One, the availability of government funding would supplement internal budgets so that the proposed research could be undertaken in a more timely manner. This was especially the case at Planar. At Photonics this was also the case because it was having a difficult time attracting venture capital for its project. Two, the National Cooperative Research and Development Act (NCRA) of 1984 lessened the potential antitrust liabilities for joint ventures that file their research intentions with the U.S. Department of Justice. Both companies believed that the proposed research would be most effectively undertaken cooperatively, so the organizational joint venture structure was desirable. The NCRA provided what the companies perceived as necessary protection against antitrust action. If subjected to antitrust action, the joint venture would be protected by the NCRA under a rule of reason that determined whether the venture improves social welfare, and the maximum financial exposure would be actual rather than treble damages.

Roles and Relationships Among Members of the Joint Venture

The Advanced Display Manufacturers of America Research Consortium (ADMARC) submitted the original research proposal to the ATP. The ADMARC was formed for the specific purpose of participating in the ATP competition. As initially structured, the head of Photonics Imaging acted as the Program Manager. Only three of the member companies were to be involved in the proposed research program: Photonics, Optical Imaging Systems (OIS), and Planar Systems, Inc.

Shortly after receiving funding from the ATP, the name of the consortium was changed to the American Display Consortium (ADC), and the organization was registered with the U.S. Department of Justice under the guidelines of the National Cooperative Research Act of 1984.

The stated objective of the project was to provide:

> broad advances in manufacturing technology ... for the flat panel display community. It will initially focus its research efforts in four areas: automated inspection, automated repair, flip chip-on-glass, and polysilicon on-glass.

Initially, Photonics was to lead the automated inspection and automated repair research, Planar the flip chip-on-glass research, and OIS the polysilicon on-glass research.

During the first year of the project, OIS was sold and could not at that time continue with its research obligations. Initially, Photonics and Planar undertook OIS's research commitments. The polysilicon on-glass effort was broadened to silicon on-glass, but the scope of the research was lessened. Throughout the research project, the membership of the ADC has changed, but not all new members in the research consortium participated in the ATP-funded joint venture. In the second year of the project, Electro Plasma, Inc.; Northrop Grumman Norden Systems; Plasmaco, Inc.; and Kent Display Systems began to share research costs. Still, Photonics and Planar remained as the research leaders of the joint venture. Each of these companies brought to the project specific expertise related to sensor and connector technology as applied to flat panels.

The research members of the joint venture compete with one another in terms of both technology and markets. Table 12.4 shows the dominant FPD technology of each member and the primary market to which that technology is applied. It should not be surprising that there are no major companies involved in this joint venture. As noted above, the major electronics companies closed or sold their flat panel divisions in the 1980s.

Table 13.4. Dominant Technology and Market of the FPD Research Members

Research Member	Technology	Market
Photonics Imaging	Plasma	Military
Planar	ELD	Industrial
Electro Plasma	Plasma	Industrial
Kent Display	Liquid Crystal	Developmental
Northrup Grumman Norden	ELD	Military
OIS-Optical	AMLCD	Military
Plasmaco	Plasma	Developmental

Research Projects and Major Technical Accomplishments

Automated Inspection

Undetected defects on a panel can result in costly repairs or even scrap if the repairs cannot be made. Manual inspection and rework of defects created in the manufacturing process can consume up to 40 percent of the total cost of production. Automated equipment now has the ability to collect data that are critical to controlling complex manufacturing processes in real time. Using such equipment in automated inspection should also be able to provide information on what to do to prevent related process problems in manufacturing. The use of automated inspection equipment and the information that it produces is expected to lower production costs and increase production yields.

The specific goals of the automated inspection project were:

(1) To design and manufacture an automatic inspection and manual repair station which would be suitable for inspecting patterns on flat display systems and give the capability of manually repairing the indicated defects, and
(2) To establish a design of systems which could be manufactured and sold to the flat panel display industry.

Specifications for an automatic inspection station were completed and a subcontract was issued to Florod in March 1993 to build an Automated Inspection Machine (AIM-1). Although a station was manufactured, significant performance problems were noticed in the fall of 1994. Personnel at the University of Michigan were used as consultants, along with the technical staff at Photonics, to help to identify and solve the technical problems with the Florod unit. As a result of the successful interaction with the University of Michigan consultants, a contract was issued to their spin-off company, Ward Synthesis, to design and build the AIM-2. Preliminary testing of AIM-2 at Photonics shows that the system has the capability to inspect successfully a wide variety of defects on various flat panel technologies.

Automated Repair

An alternative to manual repair on small, monochrome flat panels is to produce them on a high volume basis and then build yield loss into the final price. However, as display resolution and panel size increases, along with the requirement for higher quality and color, this production strategy will no longer be economically feasible. The use of automated repair is expected to lower production costs and increase production yields.

The specific goals of the automated repair project were:

(1) To establish a manufacturer of a hands-off repair system for the purpose of making both ablation repairs as well as additive repairs to FPDs, and
(2) To position pre-located defects using a database for defect type and location.

A subcontract was issued to Micron to design, assemble, and integrate an automatic repair station. The station was delivered to Photonics in December 1995 and put into use (integrated with the automatic inspection machine) in March 1996. Demonstrations of repairs to both active and passive LCD have been shown to the ADC member companies.

Technical papers related to the underlying research and operational capabilities of the repair system were delivered in 1995 at the Symposium on Electronic Imaging: Science and Technology; at the Society of Imaging Science and Technology; and at the Electronics Display Forum 95.

Flip Chip-On-Glass

Flip chip-on-glass (FCOG) is a technology used to achieve a cost effective interconnect density between a flat screen display panel and the driver of the integrated circuit (IC). The FCOG technology is important because glass may replace silicon and the printed circuit board as the common substrate for device integration. Once developed, FCOG technology will enable U.S. manufacturers of FPDs to leap-frog the current state-of-the-art for high resolution interconnect technology. As a result, production costs should decrease and reliability should increase.

The specific goals of the flip chip-on-glass project were:

(1) To evaluate and develop FCOG technologies,
(2) To evaluate the reliability and performance of the most promising FCOG technologies, and
(3) To develop cost-effective equipment for the assembly of FCOG.

This project concluded that FCOG technology was not economical at this time (according to the members of this project they were investigating a technology well ahead of the state-of-the-art). What did result was a tape automated bonding (TAB) process for mounting silicon integrated circuit (IC) dies on a reel of polyimide tape.

To explain, the TAB tape manufacturer patterns a reel of tape with the circuitry for a particular IC die. The IC manufacturer sends IC wafers to the TAB tape manufacturer and the TAB tape manufacturer bonds the individual die to the tape reel in an automated reel-to-reel process. What results is called a tape carrier package (TCP). Also in this bonding process, each individual die is tested to verify that it works properly; if a die does not work properly it is excised from the tape thus leaving a hole in the tape. The TAB tape is then sent to the display manufacturer, and the display manufacturer has automated equipment to align and bond the tape to the display glass with an anisotropic conductive adhesive. In this process, the good die are excised off of the tape, aligned to the display electrodes, and then bonded to the glass.

As part of the research of the flat panel display joint venture, Planar developed a process to bond driver ICs that were supplied by IC vendors onto a reel of TAB tape. In other words, Planar developed a process to attach the anisotropic adhesive to the glass display panel, align the excised ICs to the electrodes on the display panels, and bond the ICs to the glass panel. This process technology replaces the current elastromeric or heat seal interconnection technology between a plastic packaged IC and the display glass.

Silicon On-Glass

The scope of the silicon on-glass project was lessened because of OIS's inability to participate fully in the research. The objective of the research that was planned was to increase the level of circuit integration on the display substrate by stacking and interconnecting memory and/or decoding logic on the flat panel display line driver chips.

A contract was issued to Micro SMT to develop the desired packaging process. If successful, the FPD assembly process would be substantially improved. About one-third less area and assembly operation would be required. However, when the packages were tested at Photonics, it was determined that some of the chips could not tolerate higher voltages. Thus, this project's funding was reduced and the unused funds were directed to support the other initiatives.

New Research Projects

Funds diverted from the silicon on-glass project and funds saved on the FCOG contract totaled about $3 million. These moneys were used to fund new research projects that complemented the automated inspection and repair project and the FCOG project.

Related to automated inspection and repair, two additional research projects were undertaken in the final two years of the joint venture. The Large Area Photomaster Inspection and Repair project was led by Planar. Initially, there was no technical infrastructure for phototooling to support FPDs. This project successfully involved extending the inspection and repair technology research by Photonics toward artwork design. All FPD technologies require the use of photolithographic mark tooling to fabricate the display glass. The key feature of photomasks for FPDs, compared to ICs for example, is their size—a 24x24 inch mask compared to a 6x6 inch mask. The Defect Inspection Enhancements project was lead by Electro Plasma. Its focus was to improve manufacturing operations and its accomplishments were the introduction of new inspection methods in the manufacturing line.

Related to flip chip-on-glass, four additional projects were undertaken with the redirected funds. The goal of the Driver Interconnects Using Multi-Chip Module Laminates project was overseen by OIS. The focus of the research was to develop a method of connecting LCD drivers to the display in a way that lowered costs and improved reliability when compared to the current method of tape automated bonding (TAB). Ball Grid Array (BGA) technology was developed to accomplish this, and at present it is undergoing final environmental testing. The objective of the Development of TCP Process for High Volume, Low Cost Flat Panel Production was to establish a high volume tape carrier package (TCP) assembly to mount the TCP drivers on the display glass. TCP bonding equipment was successfully developed, qualified, and tested for reliability in the Planar FPD manufacturing line. The Driver Interconnects for Large Area Displays project was led by Northrup and Electro Plasma. The objective of this research was to identify Anisotropic Conductive Adhesives (ACAs) suitable for high-density interconnection and test them at high voltages. Also ACAs were successfully tested to military environmental conditions. Finally, the Chip-on-Glass Process Improvements project was led by Plasmaco. It had as an objective to improve the chip-on-glass manufacturing process, and it resulted in better metalization and etching processes.

PARTIAL ECONOMIC ANALYSIS OF THE JOINT VENTURE

The ATP has an evaluation program to ensure that the funded projects meet technological milestones; to determine their short-run economic impacts and, ultimately, their long-run economic impacts; and to improve the program's effectiveness. The partial economic analysis described in this section was requested by the ATP at the end of the research project. Albeit that the research had just completed, at least preliminary assessments of technical accomplishments and partial economic impacts on the companies could be made. It is still premature to evaluate systematically impacts on the rest of the economy.

As discussed in this section, even a partial economic analysis conducted at the end of the research project provides sufficient evidence to conclude that the ATP's role was successful. First, the technical accomplishments generally met or exceeded the proposed research goals, and the accomplishments were realized sooner and at a lower cost through the ATP-sponsored joint venture. Second, efforts are now underway to commercialize the developed technology. Beyond the leveraging success of the ATP program, has the overall endeavor benefited the domestic flat panel industry? Unfortunately, the verdict is still out. Although the question is the relevant one to ask and answer from the perspective of the United States as a participant in the global flat panel market, with the technology only now at the commercialization stage, one can only speculate what the answer will be.

Methodology for Data Collection

A characteristic of the research conducted in this joint venture is that research projects were for the most part conducted by single member companies, as opposed to members of the joint venture working in concert with one another on a particular project. Accordingly, it was decided through discussions with the Program Manager at Photonics that the only effective way to collect partial economic impact data was to interview participant representatives at the September 1996 end of project meeting, and at that time attempt to solicit cooperation from members, on a one-by-one basis, to participate in a follow-up electronic mail survey. The survey questions covered five areas: technical accomplishments, economic implication of ATP's funding involvement, commercialization of results, spillovers of technical knowledge, and effects on competitiveness. A limitation of this methodology is that the data collected represent opinions from participants (expressed preferences) rather than market-determined economic outcomes from the research of the joint venture (revealed preferences). The participants in the FPD joint venture are obviously those in the most informed position to discuss research accomplishments since market-based impacts will not be observed for some time.

Survey Results

Technical Accomplishments

The question posed to each identified respondent was: *Please state in lay terms the objective of the research your company undertook as part of this larger project and the major technical accomplishments realized.*

The information collected from this question was reported above as technical accomplishments.

Role of ATP Funding

The counterfactual question posed to each identified respondent was: *Would this research have taken place in your company absent the ATP funds? If NO, please estimate how many person years of effort it would take, hypothetically, to have conducted the research in house? If YES, please describe in general terms the advantages of having the ATP moneys (e.g., research would have occurred sooner than would otherwise have been the case).*

There was uniform agreement that ATP funding has increased the pace of the research, although some of the research would not have occurred in the absence of ATP funds.

Regarding automated inspection and repair, and the related projects, the unanimous opinion was that the research would not have occurred by any member of the joint venture, or by anyone else in the industry, in the absence of ATP funds. Those involved were of the opinion that if the research had been undertaken, it would have taken an additional three years to complete and an additional seven to nine person years of effort plus related equipment costs. These additional labor and equipment costs were estimated through the survey to be, in total, at least $4 million over those three years.

Regarding the flip chip-on-glass and related projects, the unanimous opinion was that this research would have been undertaken, but, "to a much lesser extent and at a much slower pace." One researcher commented: "We would have waited to see what the Japanese competitors would come out with, and then evaluate and possibly copy their interconnect technologies." Another commented that ATP funds "quickened the pace of the research by between one and two years." The Japanese industry, which dominates the FPD business, has chosen TCP packaging as the standard package, and it is the low-cost solution for driver ICs. Thus, if U.S. manufacturers are to remain competitive they must also use TCP packaging in their production processes.

As a result of ATP funds, the process technology to utilize TCP packaging exists between one and two years earlier than it would have in the absence of ATP funding. There is a cost savings implication to this hastened process technology development. It was estimated by the members of the joint venture that the use of the TCP process technology will save display manufacturers about $0.015 per line, or for the average sized panel, about $19.20 in material costs compared to the current technology. Based on a current estimate by the members of the domestic panels per year that this cost-savings estimate would apply to, the technology will save the domestic industry about $1.4 million per year. And since ATP funds hastened the development of the technology between one and two years, a first-order estimate of the industry savings from this technology over one and one-half years is about $2.1 million.

Commercialization of Results

The question posed to each identified respondent was: *Specifically, what has been commercialized by your company as a direct result of your involvement in this project? What is expected to be commercialized, and when, as a direct result of your involvement in this project? Do you have any estimate of the expected annual sales from commercialization?*

The automated inspection and repair equipment was at the demonstration point and efforts are now underway at Photonics to commercialize the product in the very near future.

The commercialization of the automated inspection and repair technology places the United States in a favorable position relative to others in the world market. For example, it was estimated that the HDTV plasma display market will be 3 million monitors per year at about $2,800 per monitor in the year 2000. That is, the market on which automated inspection and repair is initially expected to have an impact is forecast to be an $8.4 billion market by the year 2000. A conservative estimate is that U.S. companies will capture approximately 10 to 12 percent of that market, or about $924 million (using an 11 percent estimate). Currently, the size of the U.S. industry to which the technology applies is about $12.9 million. Thus, the domestic large plasma display market will increase by more than a factor of 70 during the next three years. The net cost savings from automated inspection and repair are estimated to be approximately 10 percent of the market price of the display. This means—as a conservative estimate—that the ATP-assisted development of automated inspection and repair technology will save U.S. display manufacturers approximately $92.4 million over the next three years.

Spillover Effects

The question posed to the identified respondent was: *Can you give some examples of how research conducted in another company involved in this project has been used by your company? Can you give me some instances where your research results have been shared with others in the industry that are not involved in the ATP project?*

The results from the automated inspection and repair projects have been demonstrated to both joint venture members and others in the industry. Further, the new projects emanating from the original flip chip-on-glass and silicon on-glass projects have industry-wide applicability.

Competitiveness Issues

The question posed to each identified respondent was: *Regarding the competitive position of the U.S. flat panel display industry in the world market, was the U.S. industry prior to the ATP award far behind, behind, even, ahead, or far ahead of Japan in terms of world market shares? Now, at the close of the project, where is the U.S. industry—far behind, behind, even, ahead, or far ahead of Japan in terms of world market shares?*

The general consensus was that this single ATP-funded project has helped the United States defend its current, yet small, world market position. As one respondent stated:

> The U.S. was far behind Japan in the flat panel display market [at the beginning of the project]. The U.S. is still far behind Japan but we have made some improvement in the technology available to us. It will take a little more time and more cooperation from the U.S. government to really close the gap.

CONCLUSIONS

From this chapter's assessment of the U.S. flat panel display industry two conclusions are evident. One, this case study of the U.S. flat panel display industry clearly demonstrates that, when deemed appropriate by policy officials, the U.S. innovation policy mechanism can operate swiftly. And two, when a critical industry has fallen, in terms of its technical capabilities to compete in global markets, to the level that the U.S. flat panel display industry had, it will take time before the effectiveness of any innovation policy mechanism can be fully evaluated. There is evidence to suggest that the industry has already saved on research costs and gained in time to market because of the funding support of the ATP. It is still premature to pass judgment about the long-run effect of ATP's funding leverage on the competitive vitality of the industry.

As explained in Chapter 12's evaluation of the ATP-supported printed wiring board research, for ATP projects we are for the most part evaluating research performed by the private sector with funding from the public sector, rather than publicly-performed infrastructure research in the laboratories at NIST, in particular, or in federal laboratories, in general. Nonetheless, the evaluation here of the ATP's flat panel display project focuses on the counterfactual absence of the ATP-supported project to develop an understanding of the benefits generated by the project. In comparison with our evaluations of publicly-performed infrastructure-developing research, our evaluations of ATP-supported private research projects have less often been able to ask what the counterfactual costs would be to achieve the same results without the ATP project. Instead, in the absence of the ATP project, the research is either even more unlikely to have occurred or even more likely to have occurred less completely and over a longer period of time. So, as explained in Chapter 3, for evaluation of such projects—including analogous cases for other federal laboratory projects—we try to develop understanding of not only the benefits from lower investment costs, but also the benefits because the results of the project are better—more results of higher quality achieved sooner—than would have been possible without the public/private partnership. Under ideal circumstances, with the understanding of the set of projects that would have been undertaken without ATP as compared to those actually undertaken with ATP support, and with the streams of investment benefits and costs for the counterfactual situation and the actual one, one could calculate the net present value of the ATP's support as explained by Wang (1998). In the special case where the only difference between having ATP support or not is a lowering of the investment costs, one would have the simplest counterfactual case where the evaluation metrics capture the relative investment efficiency of public-supported versus all-private investment. Wang's "incremental social return" for public sector involvement is the net present value of the incremental net benefits stream. When that net present value is positive, our counterfactual-analysis benefit-to-cost ratio is greater than one, or alternatively our counterfactual-analysis internal rate of return is greater than the opportunity cost of funds when the internal rate of return is defined. In our experience, both because the ATP projects are quite recent and because of the blend of public and private involvement, complete development of the counterfactual situation is even more difficult for ATP projects than for the projects within the laboratories at NIST.

14 TOWARD BEST PRACTICES IN PERFORMANCE EVALUATION

INTRODUCTION

In 1997 we had the honor of presenting to an Organization for Economic Co-Operation and Development (OECD) assemblage our views of best practices in performance evaluation. We chose to discuss the performance evaluation activities at the National Institute of Standards and Technology (NIST). While our experiences could have led us to focus on other federal laboratories or government agencies, we were then, and still are, of the opinion that the performance evaluation practices within the Program Office and within the Advanced Technology Program (ATP) at NIST are at the forefront. We emphasized that in Link and Scott (1998b). Hence, we have highlighted eight NIST-based case studies in this book.

SUMMARIZING THE NIST EXPERIENCE

Performance evaluation at NIST, especially as practiced in the Program Office as discussed primarily in this section, has evolved through five phases:

(1) information
(2) initiation
(3) implementation
(4) interpretation, and
(5) iteration.

We offer here these five phases as our opinion of best practices to date in U.S. agencies.

NIST *informed* internal managers of the importance of program evaluation not only to enhance managerial effectiveness but also to document the social value of the institution. This was done on a one-to-one basis with laboratory directors and in public forums and documents. To emphasize the importance of such information, note that one explicit purpose of the Government Performance and Results Act

(GPRA) of 1993 is to "help Federal managers improve service delivery," and another explicit purpose is to "improve the confidence of the American people in the capability of the Federal Government."

NIST was sensitive to the fact that management needed to be aware that their institution, like any public institution, has stakeholders and that the stakeholders pursue their own objectives. At the broadest level, the stakeholders of any U.S. government institution are the American people, but the American people only indirectly influence the annual budget of a particular institution. It is thus important to transmit information about the value of the institution to those with direct budgetary influence, and management must therefore understand and appreciate the budgetary importance of performance evaluation.

NIST *initiated* a commitment to performance evaluation by articulating an evaluation strategy. In particular, the laboratories at NIST focused on economic impacts as the key evaluation parameter. We emphasize that equally important from a performance standpoint are, on the internal side, operational efficiency, and on the external side, customer satisfaction. Within any technology-based institution, it may be the laboratory that is the relevant unit of analysis or it may be an individual research program where there are multiple research programs associated with a laboratory. If, for example, the institution-wide strategy is to evaluate each major organizational unit, then financial constraints might force the definition of the organizational unit to be encompassing. The strategy selected for the laboratories at NIST was to evaluate a representative sample of research projects; ATP, given that it is a relatively new program, selected, as we have previously described, a strategy for evaluating selected funded research projects.

Having articulated an evaluation strategy, NIST also set forth *implementation* guidelines. Educating management about performing an evaluation is not only cost effective, but also it emphasizes that performance evaluation is indeed part of the institution's culture. Part of the guidelines include an understanding of what we call the counterfactual model, compared to the Griliches/Mansfield model, as discussed in Chapter 3. Simply stated, the Griliches/Mansfield model would ask what are the benefits to NIST's investments; our counterfactual model asks what are the benefits as compared to what they would have been had the private sector made the investments. Distinguishing aspects of these alternative approaches were discussed there and summarized in Table 3.1. To avoid repetition, we offer here only Table 14.1 as a restatement of the differences in emphasis of the two models. On the left side of the table, the Griliches/Mansfield model is represented in terms of an evaluation of the direct beneficiaries and then the indirect beneficiaries via spillovers of the developed technology. On the right side of the table, the counterfactual model is represented in terms of the cost avoidance by direct beneficiaries, although as explained in Chapter 3 and then illustrated throughout the book, when the counterfactual investments cannot replicate the results of the public investments we estimate conservative lower bounds for the additional value of products or the additional cost savings attributable to the public investments, and those estimates are added to the costs avoided to get the benefits of public investment.

Regarding the economic impact assessments conducted under the guidance of the Program Office, standardized metrics for *interpretation* were agreed upon. We have discussed those metrics in Chapter 4. Within ATP, such metrics are still evolving and will likely continue to evolve as the program matures and as funded projects come to completion.

Over time, there has been learning-by-doing. Viewing performance evaluation as an *iterative* process has, in our opinion, set NIST apart from other public institutions in this dimension. For example, the set of metrics considered for laboratory evaluations has expanded over time, and within the ATP an office of evaluation has been established.

Table 14.2 summarizes the evaluation experience of NIST in terms of the five phases described just above.

Table 14.1. Alternative Approaches to the Evaluation of Outcomes

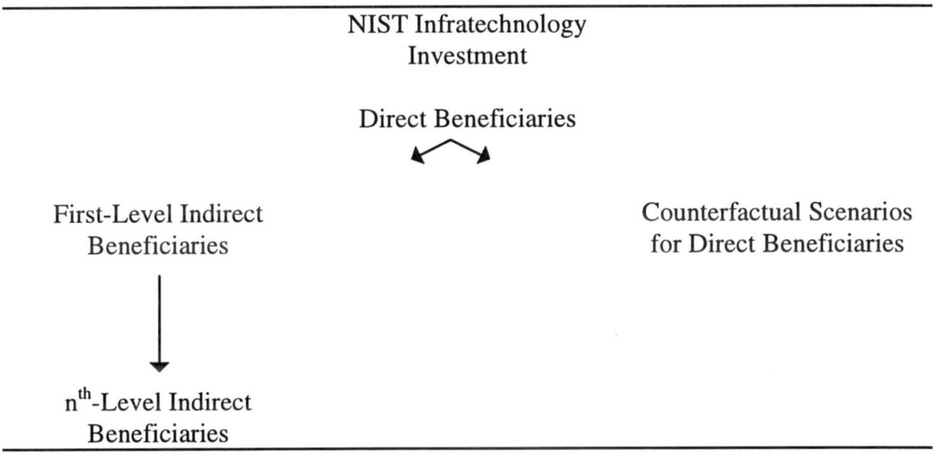

Two generalizations about the evaluation of a technology-based public institution can be posited based on the experiences at NIST. First, the apparent success at NIST is in large part because of the systematic and open manner in which performance evaluation was established. In the case of the laboratory assessments, the initial conduct of pilot studies leading to a general set of assessment guidelines certainly provided a level of comfort among the laboratory directors that these were non-threatening exercises and that they are important to the institution as a whole. In the case of ATP evaluations, the initial establishment of a plan logically led to the implementation of the plan and a venue for discussing evaluation with award recipients. In addition, the existence of the plan provided a platform from which ATP could justify its mission in the current political environment that was attempting to cut federal support of industrial research.

Table 14.2. Summary of Performance Evaluation Experiences at NIST

Characteristics	Laboratory Evaluations	ATP Evaluations
Information	Effectively informed laboratory directors about the managerial importance and political realities of performance evaluation	Effectively informed staff about the political realities of performance evaluation but are only beginning to inform award recipients of the same because of the newness of the program
Initiation	Pilot evaluation projects were undertaken to articulate the evaluation strategy of conducting economic impact assessments at the project level within each laboratory	At the forefront of government agencies in establishing *a priori* an evaluation plan and making efforts to implement it in real time
Implementation	Published NIST guidelines on the conduct of economic impact assessment; Director of NIST held open information meetings with NIST staff	Adopted a multifaceted evaluation program that is broader than economic impact assessment; involved large segments of the academic community to assist
Interpretation	Adopted initial interpretative metrics and have undertaken efforts to educate laboratory directors on the meaning and usefulness of these metrics	Interpretation of evaluation results is evolving because of the newness of the program; collection of qualitative information from awardees to interpret to political constituents the importance of the program to the industrial community
Iteration	Subsequent economic impact assessments are more encompassing and have institutionalized additional metrics	ATP is supporting research by academics into evaluation methods applicable to its program

Second, neither the laboratory nor ATP performance evaluation efforts have to date been able to institutionalize the collection of assessment/evaluation-related data in real time. Certainly, it is desirable to have laboratory programs collecting impact information in real time through their normal interactions with their industrial constituents. Such an activity would represent a change in the culture of the laboratories' mode of interaction, as it would that of any technology-based institution. Likewise, ATP has not yet been successful, although the newness of the program would imply that they could not yet have been successful, in having award recipients involved in the identification of evaluation-related data in real time, although according to Powell (1998) progress is being made.

TOWARD BEST PRACTICES IN PERFORMANCE EVALUATION

The successful experience in performance evaluation at NIST suggests one possible set of characteristics for best practices applicable to any technology-based public institution.

One, instill an institutional belief that performance evaluation is important. Management must be educated about the overall gains to the institution from on-going program evaluation (and they must also be convinced that performance evaluation is not the first step toward budget reallocation, but rather a response to public accountability criteria). Such an *a priori* education is necessary for establishing evaluation as a part of the culture of the institution and its technology planning process.

Two, select a standardized method for conducting performance evaluation. The institution must conduct pilot evaluations as demonstrations of how to apply evaluation methods and how to learn from one evaluation exercise to the next. Subsequently, the selected standardized method is institutionalized. The method must be clearly articulated to management and reasonable in terms of implementation. Likewise, the related evaluation metrics must correspond to accepted evaluation practices, and, perhaps most important, they must be easily understood by the broader evaluation community.

And three, execute performance evaluations. Staring into the future is what technology planning is all about; performance evaluation is a key to gaining understanding necessary for successful technology planning. Because no one's crystal ball is thoroughly accurate, the best one can hope for is systematic and informed judgment that can be clearly explained and articulated. Technology planning that is grounded in ongoing evaluation provides two important qualities: it enables the institution to explain its mission and goals to an internal and external audience of stakeholders; and, as important, it allows the institution in time to understand errors, to learn from them, and to incorporate that knowledge into the planning and evaluation cycle.

REFERENCES

Abraham, Thomas. "U.S. Advanced Ceramics Market Growth Continues," *Ceramic Industry*, 1996.

Bosch, John A. *Coordinate Measuring Machines and Systems*, New York: Marcel Decker, 1995.

Bozeman, Barry and Julia Melkers. *Evaluating R&D Impacts: Methods and Practice*, Norwell, Mass.: Kluwer Academic Publishers, 1993.

Braswell, Arnold. "Testimony Before the Subcommittee on Oversight and Investigations of the Committee on Energy and Commerce," House of Representatives, May 15, 1989.

Burns, G.W. "Temperature-Electromotive Force Reference Functions and Tables for the Letter-Designated Thermocouple Types Based on the ITS-90," NIST Monograph 175, 1993.

Burns, G.W. and M.G. Scroger. "The Calibration of Thermocouples and Thermocouple Materials," NIST Special Publication 250-35, 1989.

Cochrane, Rexmond C. *Measures for Progress: A History of the National Bureau of Standards*, Washington, D.C.: U.S. Government Printing Office, 1966.

Cogan, Douglas G. *Stones in a Glass House: CFCs and Ozone Depletion,* Washington, D.C.: Investor Responsibility Research Center, Inc., 1988.

Collins, Eileen. "Performance Reporting in Federal Management Reform," National Science Foundation Special Report, mimeographed, 1997.

Council on Competitiveness. *Critical Technologies Update 1994*, Washington, D.C.: Council on Competitiveness, 1994.

Council on Competitiveness. *Gaining New Ground: Technology Priorities for America's Future*, Washington, D.C.: Council on Competitiveness, 1991.

Cozzens, Susan E. "Assessment of Fundamental Science Programs in the Context of the Government Performance and Results Act (GPRA)," Washington, D.C.: Critical Technologies Institute, 1995.

Flamm, Kenneth S. "Flat-Panel Displays: Catalyzing a U.S. Industry," *Issues in Science and Technology*, 1994.

Flatt, Michael. *Printed Circuit Board Basics*, 2nd edition, San Francisco: Miller Freemen Books, 1992.

Georghiou, Luke. "Research Evaluation in European National Science and Technology Systems," *Research Evaluation*, 1995.

Griliches, Zvi. "Research Costs and Social Returns: Hybrid Corn and Related Innovations," *Journal of Political Economy*, 1958.

Hess, Pamela. "Sharpe Will Open Domestic Production Facility for AMLCDs in October," *Inside the Pentagon*, 1994.

Hillstrom, Kevin. *Encyclopedia of American Industries, Volume 1: Manufacturing Industries*, New York: Gale Research, Inc., 1994.

Hocken, Robert J. "Software Correction of Precision Machines," NIST Final Report 60NANB2D1214, 1993.

Institute for Interconnecting and Packaging Electronic Circuits, TMRC. *Analysis of the Market: Rigid Printed Wiring Boards and Related Materials for the Year 1991.* Lincolnwood, Ill.: Institute for Interconnecting and Packaging Electronic Chips, 1992.

Institute for Interconnecting and Packaging Electronic Circuits, TMRC. *Analysis of the Market: Rigid Printed Wiring Boards and Related Materials for the Year 1994.* Lincolnwood, Ill.: Institute for Interconnecting and Packaging Electronic Chips, 1995a.

Institute for Interconnecting and Packaging Electronic Circuits, TMRC. Minutes from the May 21-23, 1995, meeting in Washington, D.C., 1995b.

Kostoff, Ronald. "Science and Technology Metrics," Office of Naval Research, mimeographed, 1998.

Krishna, Kala and Marie Thursby. "Wither Flat Panel Displays?" NBER Working Paper 5415, 1996.

Leech, David P. and Albert N. Link. "The Economic Impacts of NIST's Software Error Compensation Research," NIST Planning Report 96-2, 1996.

Link, Albert N. "Advanced Technology Program Case Study: Early Stage Impacts of the Printed Wiring Board Research Joint Venture, Assessed at Project End," NIST Report GCR 97-722, 1997.

Link, Albert N. "Economic Impact Assessments: Guidelines for Conducting and Interpreting Assessment Studies," NIST Planning Report 96-1, 1996a.

Link, Albert N. "Evaluating the Advanced Technology Program: A Preliminary Assessment of Economic Impacts," *International Journal of Technology Management*, 1993.

Link, Albert N. *Evaluating Public Sector Research and Development*, New York: Praeger Publishers, 1996b.

Link, Albert N. "The U.S. Display Consortium: Analysis of a Public/Private Partnership," *Industry and Innovation*, 1998.

Link, Albert N. and John T. Scott. "Assessing the Infrastructural Needs of a Technology-Based Service Sector: A New Approach to Technology Policy Planning" *STI Review,* 1998a.

Link, Albert N. and John T. Scott. "Evaluating Technology-Based Public Institutions: Lessons from the National Institute of Standards and Technology," in *Policy Evaluation in Innovation and Technology*, edited by G. Papaconstantinou, Paris: OECD, 1998b.

McLoughlin, Glenn J. and Richard M. Nunno. "Flat Panel Display Technology: What Is the Federal Role?" Congressional Research Service Report, 1995.

Mansfield, Edwin, John Rapoport, Anthony Romeo, Samuel Wagner, and George Beardsley. "Social and Private Rates of Return from Industrial Innovations," *Quarterly Journal of Economics*, 1977.

Marx, Michael L., Albert N. Link, and John T. Scott. "Economic Assessment of the NIST Ceramic Phase Diagram Program," NIST Planning Report 98-3, 1998.

Marx, Michael L., Albert N. Link, and John T. Scott. "Economic Assessment of the NIST Thermocouple Calibration Program," NIST Planning Report 97-1, 1997.

National Science and Technology Council. "Assessing Fundamental Science," Washington, D.C.: National Science and Technology Council, 1996.

Office of Management and Budget. "Circular No. A-94: Guidelines and Discount Rates for Benefit-Cost Analysis of Federal Programs," Washington, D.C., 1992.

Powell, Jeanne W. "Pathways to National Economic Benefits from ATP-Funded Technologies," *Journal of Technology Transfer*, 1998.

Rosenberg, Nathan. *Technology and American Economic Growth*, New York: Sharp, 1972.

Ruegg, Rosalie. "The Advanced Technology Program, Its Evaluation Plan, and Progress in Implementation," *Journal of Technology Transfer*, 1998.

Ruegg, Rosalie T. and Harold E. Marshall. *Building Economics: Theory and Practice,* New York: Van Nostrand Reinhold, 1990.

Saleh, B.E.A. and M.C. Teich. "Fundamentals of Photonics," unpublished manuscript, 1990.

Scherer, F.M. "The Welfare Economics of Product Variety: An Application to the Ready-to-Eat Cereals Industry," *Journal of Industrial Economics*, 1979.

Shedlick, Matthew T., Albert N. Link, and John T. Scott. "Economic Assessment of the NIST Alternative Refrigerants Research Program," NIST Planning Report 98-1, 1998.

Solar Energy Research Institute. "Basic Photovoltaic Principles and Methods," SERI/SP-290-1448, 1982.

Tassey, Gregory. "Lessons Learned about the Methodology of Economic Impact Studies: The NIST Experience," *Evaluation and Program Planning,* forthcoming.

Trajtenberg, Manual. *Economic Analysis of Product Innovation: The Case of CT Scanners*, Cambridge, Mass.: Harvard University Press, 1990.

U.S. Department of Defense. *Special Technology Area Review on Flat Panel Displays*, Washington, D.C.: U.S. Department of Defense, 1993.

U.S. Department of Defense. *National Flat Panel Display Initiative: Summary and Overview*, Washington, D.C.: U.S. Department of Defense, 1994.

Wang, Andrew J. "Key Concepts in Evaluating Outcomes of ATP Funding of Medical Technologies," *Journal of Technology Transfer*, 1998.

INDEX